CD&I (C 116)

2 May 2016

ERRATUM

to

MCWP 3-42.1

UNMANNED AIRCRAFT SYSTEMS OPERATIONS

1. Change all instances of MCWP 3-42.1, *Unmanned Aircraft Systems Operations*, to MCWP 3-20.5, *Unmanned Aircraft Systems Operations*.

2. File this transmittal sheet in the front of this publication.

PCN 143 000141 80

DEPARTMENT OF THE NAVY
Headquarters United States Marine Corps
Washington, D.C. 20350-3000

09 December 2015

FOREWORD

Marine Corps Warfighting Publication (MCWP) 3-42.1, *Unmanned Aircraft Systems Operations*, defines how and why unmanned aircraft systems (UASs) are operated in support of the Marine air-ground task force (MAGTF). This publication provides UAS employment guidance and considerations to commanders, their staffs, and UAS personnel. It addresses planning and coordination requirements, employment concepts, command and support relationships, request procedures, and unmanned aircraft capabilities.

Combat in Operation Iraqi Freedom and Operation Enduring Freedom has emphasized the need to improve timeliness and accuracy of battlefield information and derived intelligence to improve the essential fire and maneuver capabilities of Marine ground forces in all operational environments.Traditional MAGTF fires and emerging capabilities that can influence and shape the operating environment must be available 24 hours a day, 7 days a week, and under all weather conditions. They must be able to rapidly and precisely engage fleeting opportunities found in a range of military operations while supporting the concept of maneuver warfare. Unmanned aircraft systems are the persistent link and combat multiplier that allow the MAGTF to improve its situational awareness and achieve timely combined arms effectiveness.

Unmanned aircraft systems include the necessary equipment, data communications links, and personnel to control and employ an unmanned aircraft. Unmanned aircraft can be a rotary-wing, fixed-wing, or lighter-than-air aircraft capable of flight without an on-board crew. For the purposes of this publication, all unmanned aircraft will be considered recoverable, even if they are occasionally expended during actual combat operations. Unmanned aircraft may be operated remotely or autonomously and can carry a lethal or nonlethal payload.

This publication supersedes MCWP 3-42.1, *Unmanned Aerial Vehicle Operations*, dated 14 August 2003.

Reviewed and approved this date.

BY DIRECTION OF THE COMMANDANT OF THE MARINE CORPS

ROBERT S. WALSH
Lieutenant General, U.S. Marine Corps
Deputy Commandant for Combat Development and Integration

Publication Control Number: 143 000141 00

DISTRIBUTION STATEMENT A: Approved for public release; distribution is unlimited.

Table of Contents

Chapter 1. Fundamentals

Historical Background 1-1
Components 1-2
    Unmanned Aircraft 1-3
    Payload 1-3
    Control Element 1-3
    Communications 1-3
    Support Element 1-3
Categories 1-3
Interoperability Levels 1-4
Factors Unique to Unmanned Aircraft Systems 1-5
    Human Factors 1-5
    Endurance 1-5
    Multiple Communications Paths 1-5
    Multiple Vulnerability Points 1-6
    Sensor Reliance 1-6
    Meteorological Effects 1-6
A Family of Systems Concept of Operations 1-6
Roles in the Six Functions of Marine Aviation 1-7
    Antiair Warfare 1-7
    Electronic Warfare 1-7
    Offensive Air Support 1-8
    Air Reconnaissance 1-8
    Assault Support 1-8
    Control of Aircraft and Missiles 1-9

Chapter 2. Organization

MAGTF Maneuver Units 2-1
Marine Unmanned Aerial Vehicle Squadrons 2-2
    RQ-7B Shadow 2-3
    RQ-21A Blackjack 2-4
Task Organization of Marine Unmanned Aerial Vehicle Squadron Detachments 2-5

Chapter 3. Planning

Principles for Effective Employment 3-1
    Plan Early and Continuously..3-1
    Maximize Integration 3-1
    Ensure Unity of Command...3-3
Tactical Planning Considerations 3-4
    Transfer of Control...3-5
    Duty Day 3-5
    Emergency Planning 3-6
    Vulnerability 3-6
    Route Planning 3-6
    Deceptive Routing..3-6
    Terminal Area Airspace Planning 3-7
Tasking 3-7
    Organic Direct Support Tasking 3-7
    Aviation Tasking..3-7
    Dynamic Tasking 3-8
    Electronic Warfare Tasking 3-8
Airspace Coordination 3-10
Considerations for Effective Operations 3-11
    Ground Support Planning...3-11
    Threats...3-11
    Airspace 3-11
    Weather 3-12
    Communications 3-12
    Contingencies 3-16

Chapter 4. Operations

Operational Roles 4-1
Concept of Operations and Tactics...4-2
    Surveillance and Reconnaissance for Maneuver Units...4-2
    Movement Operations (Launch, Displace, and Recover) 4-2
    Single-Site Operations 4-2
Battlespace Coordination..4-3
    Time-Sensitive Targets 4-3
    Transfer of Control During Mission Execution 4-3

Reconnaissance Information and Intelligence Management 4-3

    Information and Intelligence 4-4

    The Intelligence Cycle and the Tasking, Processing and Exploitation,

        and Dissemination Process 4-5

    Imagery Intelligence... 4-6

Imagery Storage and Archiving.. 4-8

Electronic Warfare Operations With Appropriate Payloads 4-8

Chapter 5. Employment

Employment Concepts and Considerations 5-1

    Transportation Requirements 5-1

    Supply Support.. 5-1

    Engineer Support.. 5-1

    Power Generation... 5-2

Employment Considerations.. 5-2

    Operating Sites 5-2

    Employment Configurations 5-3

    Control Station Transfer... 5-4

Marine Unmanned Aerial Vehicle Squadron Mission Execution 5-4

    Flight Brief... 5-4

    Launch/Takeoff.. 5-4

    Recovery 5-4

Integration With Joint or Combined Forces 5-5

Future Employment 5-5

Glossary

References and Related Publications

To Our Readers

CHAPTER 1
FUNDAMENTALS

HISTORICAL BACKGROUND

Unmanned aircraft have been used by militaries since World War I when the British used modified biplanes as remotely piloted aerial torpedoes. In the 1950s and 1960s, the US Navy, Marine Corps, and Air Force operated unmanned systems, some of which were flown for reconnaissance over North Vietnam. The Marine Corps first conducted successful, sustained unmanned aerial vehicle (UAV) operations in the early 1980s when the RQ-2B Pioneer was used as a spotting platform for naval gunfire and artillery. Common terminology changed in 2008 from UAV to unmanned aircraft system (UAS), as the UAV itself was only one component of the entire system. RQ-2B Pioneer systems were initially attached to the 10th Marine Artillery Regiment, Target Acquisition Battery. In 1984, the Navy flew Pioneer systems to support naval gunfire operations off the coast of Lebanon. As the role of UASs expanded, the Marine Corps began to employ Pioneer as a designated reconnaissance asset, thus ending its exclusive role as a spotting platform. The Pioneer systems were removed from the artillery regiments and established as distinct UAS units within the Marine Division, Headquarters Battalion shortly thereafter. Remotely piloted vehicle (RPV) platoons and later RPV companies were formed and assigned to the surveillance, reconnaissance, and intelligence groups within the Marine amphibious force. Two RPV companies conducted the first sustained combat operations with Pioneer during Operation Desert Shield and Operation Desert Storm, flying over 1,200 combat hours.

During Operation Desert Storm, Pioneer conducted hundreds of reconnaissance missions, frequently observing enemy activity and locations such as troop movements, artillery positions, armored formations, surface-to-surface missiles, and air defense sites. Shortly after Operation Desert Storm, 2d RPV Company flew in support of Operation Provide Comfort, providing surveillance and locating pockets of Kurdish refugees.

In January 1996, RPV companies were redesignated as Marine unmanned aerial vehicle squadrons (VMUs), transferred to the aviation combat element (ACE), and reorganized under the Marine aircraft wing (MAW). This improved both maintenance practices and the integration of unmanned aircraft into the larger tactical air picture. In 1996, VMU-1 deployed to Bosnia and Herzegovina in support of Operation Joint Endeavor, where it supported North Atlantic Treaty Organization (NATO) peacekeeping operations. For the remainder of the 1990s, VMU-1 and VMU-2 trained and supported several counterdrug missions along the southern border of the United States.

In the late 1990s, the Marine Corps increased development and deployment of small, hand-launched UASs. By 2001, the Marine Corps was employing the RQ-14A Dragon Eye at the small-unit level for short-range, tactical air reconnaissance. Over 400 Dragon Eye systems were fielded to battalion-level ground units across the Marine Corps.

In February 2003, VMU-1 and VMU-2—then comprising the entirety of the Marine Corps' UAS capability—deployed to Kuwait in support of Operation Enduring Freedom (OEF) and later to Iraq in support of Operation Iraqi Freedom (OIF) and, within Operation OIF, Operation Phantom Fury. For the next seven years, the two VMUs continuously rotated between Operations OIF and OEF, providing vital intelligence on insurgent activity, spotting for artillery fire, coordinating airstrikes, and providing battle damage assessment.

Following the success of UASs in combat, the Marine Corps contracted the SE-20 ScanEagle, a commercial UAS, to meet the growing demand for air reconnaissance in Operations OIF and OEF. To modernize and grow the force, the Marine Corps replaced the Dragon Eye with the RQ-11B Raven Digital Data Link (DDL), a similar but significantly improved hand-launched UAS. In 2007, the Marine Corps began fielding RQ-7B Shadow systems to replace the aging RQ-2B Pioneers, assigning three RQ-7B systems to each VMU. Due to the high operational tempo of VMU-1 and VMU-2, the Marine Corps activated a third active duty squadron, VMU-3, in 2008. In 2011, VMU-4 was activated to ensure that 4th MAW was equipped with a UAS capability.

During Operation OEF, US forces saw an increased use of improvised explosive devices within the operational area, which resulted in a joint urgent operational needs statement to increase air logistical support missions while reducing convoy traffic. In response, the Marine Corps contracted the development of two cargo resupply UASs in 2011. By mid-2014, the two rotary-wing platforms had flown over 2,000 hours, externally transporting over four million pounds of cargo to and from austere, outlying forward operating bases. Today, UASs continue to support the Marine air-ground task force (MAGTF) in multiple theaters during both major combat and contingency operations.

COMPONENTS

Joint Publication (JP) 3-52, *Joint Airspace Control*, defines a UAS as a system whose components include the necessary equipment, network, and personnel to control an unmanned aircraft. Marine Corps UASs are distinguished from munitions, decoys, and other entities capable of unmanned flight in that they are generally intended for recovery and reuse after each mission. There are five components common to all UASs: unmanned aircraft, payload, control element, communications, and support element. See Marine Corps Reference Publication (MCRP) 3-42.1A, *Multi-Service Tactics, Techniques, and Procedures for the Tactical Employment of Unmanned Aircraft Systems*, for more information.

Unmanned Aircraft

Unmanned aircraft are rotary-wing, fixed-wing, or lighter-than-air vehicles capable of flight without an on-board crew. The unmanned aircraft includes the aircraft and its integrated equipment (i.e., propulsion, avionics, fuel, navigation, and on-board communications systems).

Payload

Payloads may include sensors, communications relays, and weapons. The numbers and types of payloads present will affect the performance characteristics of most UASs.

Control Element

The control element (whether ground-based, sea-based, or airborne) may handle multiple mission aspects, such as mission planning and execution, payload control, and communications. The unmanned aircraft operator is physically located at the primary UAS control element referred to as the ground control station (GCS). The GCS can be a laptop computer, large control van, shipboard module, or fixed facility. It can also be located on-board airborne platforms to enable control from manned aircraft. Some GCSs can allow one pilot or operator to control multiple unmanned aircraft. For some larger UASs, the GCS may be geographically separated from the unmanned aircraft launch and recovery site (LRS) and may be located outside the area of operations. Additionally, sensor operators control wide-area airborne surveillance and most signals intelligence (SIGINT) sensors at a location geographically separated from the primary UAS control element.

Communications.

All communications among the unmanned aircraft, UAS control element, and supported unit occur via voice and data link. The unmanned aircraft may use line-of-sight (LOS) or beyond-line-of-sight communications. Unmanned aircraft data links can directly supply the warfighter with imagery and associated metadata via direct LOS downlink to a remote video terminal (RVT). Distributed common ground systems (DCGSs), the Global Broadcast Service, or the unmanned aircraft itself can directly (e.g., RVT) transmit data products via the Department of Defense Information Network.

Support Element

Like manned aircraft, UASs require logistic support. The UAS support element includes the equipment to deploy, transport, maintain, launch, and recover the unmanned aircraft and enable its communications.

CATEGORIES

The Department of Defense (DOD) categorizes all unmanned aircraft into one of five groups based on three enduring attributes: maximum gross takeoff weight, normal operating altitude, and speed (see table 1-1). Group categories are based exclusively on characteristics of the unmanned aircraft itself and without regard for the composition or disposition of the remainder of the system.

Unmanned aircraft group categories were established and approved by the Joint Staff in November 2008 as a means to more easily establish joint UAS policy and to facilitate DOD interaction with the Department of Transportation and Federal Aviation Administration.

Table 1-1. Unmanned Aircraft Group Categories.

UA Category	Maximum Gross Takeoff Weight (pounds)	Normal Operating Altitude (feet)	Speed (knots indicated airspeed)
Group 1	0–20	< 1,200 AGL	< 100
Group 2	21–55	< 3,500 AGL	< 250
Group 3	56–1,320	< 18,000 MSL	
Group 4	> 1,320		Any airspeed
Group 5		> 18,000 MSL	

Legend
MSL—mean sea level
UA—unmanned aircraft

Group 1 consists of small unmanned aircraft systems (SUASs) that are operated by all elements of the MAGTF; command, ground, aviation, and logistics. Unmanned aircraft systems in groups 2 through 5 are operated by the VMUs to serve as an integral component of a task-organized ACE in support of MAGTFs of any size or type.

INTEROPERABILITY LEVELS

Table 1-2 identifies five levels of UAS interoperability. To be effective, UASs must possess the ability to operate with other Services and other nations, specifically NATO member nations. Compliance with NATO Standardization Agreement (STANAG) 4586, *Standard Interfaces of UAV Control System (UCS) for NATO UAV Interoperability*, allows NATO member nations to jointly support military operations using their own UAS and GCS equipment, increases interoperability, and allows data and information processed by member nation UASs to be shared in real time through common ground interfaces. See STANAG 4586 for detailed information.

Table 1-2. Interoperability Levels.

Level 1	Indirect receipt/transmission of UAS-related payload data
Level 2	Direct receipt of ISR data where "direct" covers reception of the UAS payload data by the unmanned control system when it has direct communication with the UAS
Level 3	Control and monitoring of the UAS payload in addition to direct receipt of ISR and other data
Level 4	Control and monitoring of the UAS, less launch and recovery capability
Level 5	Control and monitoring of the UAS, including launch and recovery capability

FACTORS UNIQUE TO UNMANNED AIRCRAFT SYSTEMS

Unmanned aircraft systems have unique capabilities that make them essential assets to the MAGTF. Like all aviation assets, they have limitations specific to their type, model, and series. When supported commanders and staff planners consider employing UASs as assets and integrating them into their scheme of maneuver, it is more important they consider factors that are unique to the particular type of aircraft than to weigh capabilities against limitations. In some situations, a specific factor unique to UASs may enable the aircraft to perform tasks that other aircraft cannot; in other situations, the same factor may pose limitations.

Human Factors
One of the key benefits to employing a UAS is the risk to the UAS crew in flight is significantly reduced or eliminated. Physical factors that affect manned aircrews such as hypoxia or g-force have no effect on UAS crews. Human risk factors, however, are still important for UAS crew consideration, even though they are less affected by physical factors. Additionally, mission planners must always consider risks to other aircraft, personnel, equipment, and facilities. Because the crew is not physically located inside the cockpit, some facets of UAS operation may be more difficult. For example, the UAS crew is unable to simply look outside the cockpit or experience the physical "seat of your pants" effects, which are critical sensory inputs to manned aviation. Conversely, remote operation negates the requirement for such sensory inputs, allowing the UAS flight control computer to interpret environmental effects upon the aircraft and respond accordingly. In most cases, the system's computer is more effective than a human in interpreting and correcting these effects. Maintaining an appropriate state of alert and situational awareness over long-duration flights is a constant challenge. Advanced technology in automated flight control and mission autonomy reduces the cost and time to train operators. However, instilling flight discipline, adhering to standard aviation flight rules, and developing good aviation practices—all devoid of a self-preservation mindset—are unique and critical challenges in the development of UAS crews.

Endurance
Unmanned aircraft systems typically have a significantly longer endurance than their manned counterparts. They can provide uninterrupted support to tactical missions and sequentially support multiple missions with a single aircraft. Additionally, UASs allow for hot seating (i.e., changing crews mid-mission), which maximizes the aircraft's endurance while preserving alertness and discipline among the crew when a single sortie is tasked to support multiple, sequential missions. For UASs, however, endurance does not necessarily increase combat range. Unmanned aircraft systems generally transit at slower speeds than manned aircraft and may require longer transit times to reach their operating areas, which may reduce available time on station.

Multiple Communications Paths
Unmanned aircraft systems typically possess multiple communications paths between their aircrew on the ground and the aircraft. Many UASs have a large capacity for data communications in addition to single-channel radio and satellite communications (SATCOM). A UAS can act as a radio and data communications bridge between units depending on its payload, off-board system, and configuration. Unmanned aircraft systems equipped with a communications relay payload

allow crews to communicate through the aircraft to supported units. Adding a new communications path to a UAS may simply require an off-board system, which can be installed rapidly and without modification to the aircraft. Before installing additional communications systems, planners and operators must consider the collective effect of all systems on available bandwidth. Additionally, UAS crews may have the option of face-to-face communication with the supported unit or the ability to fully utilize ground-based communications networks.

Multiple Vulnerability Points

Specific information on UAS vulnerabilities is classified; however, when supported units, staffs, and UAS planners consider threats, they must not limit considerations exclusively to the aircraft. Threats to the entire system and the associated data links must always be considered during planning.

Sensor Reliance

Unmanned aircraft system crews are exclusively reliant upon on-board and off-board sensors and systems for situational awareness once the unmanned aircraft is beyond visual range of the crew. Unmanned aircraft system crews lack the ability to visually observe, but this does not mean they possess lesser situational awareness than manned aircraft crews. Off-board systems can establish a reliable air and ground picture that provides UAS crews with situational awareness superior to that of a manned aircraft operating under visual flight rules in the same tactical objective area. Unmanned aircraft automation reduces crew task saturation and mission cross-check times, which may allow crews to process more information than their manned counterparts.

Meteorological Effects

Wind and precipitation have a greater effect on many UASs, as they tend to be smaller, lighter, and slower than manned aircraft. High or gusty wind conditions can adversely affect launch and recovery operations and increase fuel consumption, adversely affecting mission time. Most unmanned aircraft cannot operate in icing conditions, and most also lack watertight airframe integrity, preventing operations in even light to moderate rain.

A FAMILY OF SYSTEMS CONCEPT OF OPERATIONS

To support MAGTF operations throughout the range of military operations, the Marine Corps employs its organic UASs as a family of systems, which performs overlapping and complementary tactical functions. These components of the Marine Corps family of UASs are employed across each level of the MAGTF with a common command and control (C2) architecture. Each UAS within the family of systems is organized within the table of equipment of a specific unit, normally assigned according to unmanned aircraft group category.

Higher echelons of MAGTF commands will possess fewer UASs, but their UASs will have increased tactical capabilities. Conversely, lower echelons will possess UASs with lesser capabilities but have more in number, therefore providing increased persistence.

Organizing the family of UASs in support of different echelons within the MAGTF—

- Maximizes asset coverage while minimizing capability gaps.
- Optimizes the capabilities of different UASs at the appropriate echelon.
- Simplifies tasking.
- Maximizes mutual support while reducing redundant tasking.
- Facilitates UAS integration within the ACE at the appropriate echelon (squadron, aircraft group, or aircraft wing).
- Task-organizes UAS units for deployment.
- Provides commanders at all levels with increased, persistent aviation support capabilities and tactical battlespace situational awareness.

ROLES IN THE SIX FUNCTIONS OF MARINE AVIATION

The Marine Corps achieves combined arms synergy by coordinating and organizing all of its efforts into six warfighting functions: command and control, maneuver, fires, intelligence, logistics, and force protection. Marine Corps Warfighting Publication (MCWP) 3-2, *Aviation Operations*, details how the tasks of Marine aviation fall into six integrated functional areas based on Marine aviation capabilities. These six functional areas contribute significantly to the six warfighting functions. Figure 1-1, on page 1-8, shows how Marine Corps UASs are assigned mission-essential tasks within five of the six functions of Marine aviation in support of five of the six warfighting functions. As technology continues to rapidly advance, Marine Corps UASs will perform roles of greater depth and breadth within Marine aviation. The following subparagraphs discuss each of the six functions of Marine aviation in relation to UAS task contributions.

Antiair Warfare

Antiair warfare (AAW) refers to the actions used to destroy the enemy air and missile threat or reduce it to an acceptable level. Antiair warfare supports the force protection warfighting function. The primary purpose of AAW is to gain and maintain the required degree of air superiority, permitting the conduct of operations without prohibitive interference by opposing air and missile forces. Unmanned aircraft systems contribute to AAW by performing offensive AAW. Offensive AAW are operations conducted against enemy air assets and air defense systems before they can be launched or assume an attacking role. Offensive AAW includes suppression of enemy air defenses.

Electronic Warfare

Electronic warfare is any military action involving the use of the electromagnetic spectrum (EMS) and directed energy to control the EMS or to attack the enemy. In joint doctrine, electronic warfare is a subset of electromagnetic spectrum operations (EMSO) and includes electromagnetic spectrum management operations. Electronic warfare supports the force protection, fires, and intelligence warfighting functions. Marine Corps UASs provide support to two of the three major subdivisions of electronic warfare: electronic attack and electronic warfare support.

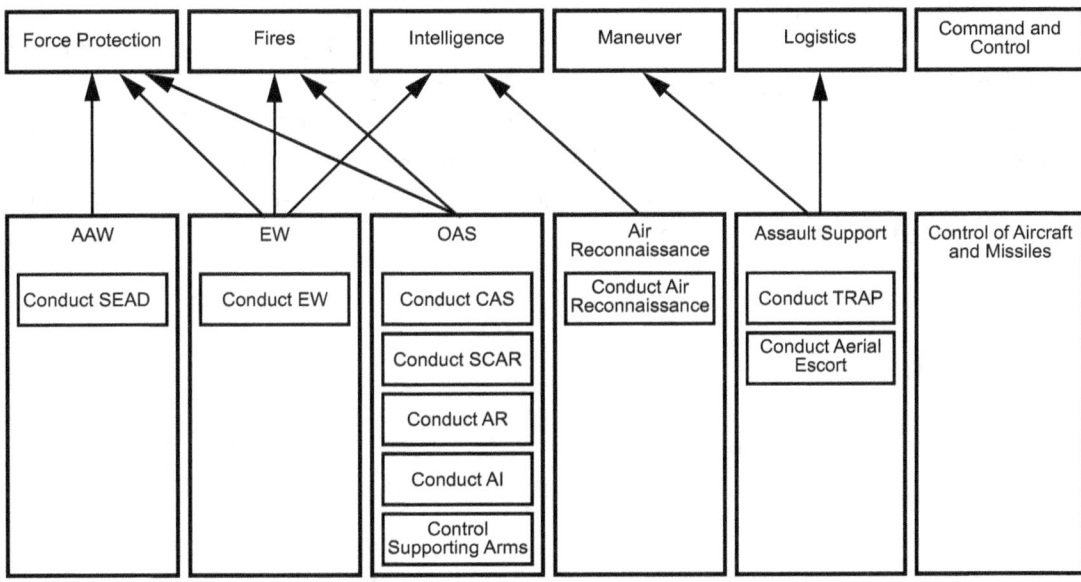

Marine Unmanned Aerial Vehicle Squadron Mission-Essential Tasks

LEGEND

AI	airborne interdiction
AR	air refueling
EW	electronic warfare
OAS	offensive air support
SEAD	suppression of enemy air defenses
TRAP	tactical recovery of aircraft and personnel

**Figure 1-1. Marine Corps Unmanned Aircraft
System Support to the Six Warfighting Functions.**

Offensive Air Support

Offensive air support involves air operations conducted against installations, facilities, and personnel in order to directly assist in the attainment of MAGTF objectives by destroying enemy resources or isolating enemy military forces. Its primary support of the warfighting function is to provide fires and force protection through close air support (CAS) and deep air support. Marine Corps UASs support CAS and all three types of deep air support missions: armed reconnaissance, air interdiction, and strike coordination and reconnaissance (SCAR).

Air Reconnaissance

This function employs visual observation and/or sensors in aerial vehicles to acquire intelligence information. It supports the intelligence warfighting function and is employed tactically, operationally, and strategically. The three types of air reconnaissance are visual, multisensor imagery, and electronic. Marine Corps UASs primarily support multisensory imagery reconnaissance.

Assault Support

Assault support contributes to the warfighting functions of maneuver and logistics. Maneuver warfare demands rapid, flexible maneuverability to achieve a decision. Marine Corps UASs support this function by providing aviation support to tactical recovery of aircraft and personnel and air logistical support. Marine Corps UASs also support this function by performing aerial escort.

Control of Aircraft and Missiles

This function integrates the other five functions of Marine aviation by providing the commander with the ability to exercise C2 authority over Marine aviation assets. The ACE commander maintains centralized command, while control is decentralized and executed through the Marine air command and control system. Because UASs are not Marine air command and control system assets and are not tasked to perform air control or air direction, they do not directly contribute to the control of aircraft and missiles function.

CHAPTER 2
ORGANIZATION

The Marine Corps family of UASs provides each level of the MAGTF with a tactical, organic, interoperable, integrated, and tailored battlespace awareness and force application capability and enables enhanced command and control throughout the range of military operations. The larger, more capable systems support higher levels of command; the smaller but more numerous systems directly support lower tactical units.

MAGTF MANEUVER UNITS

Small unmanned aircraft systems are particularly well suited to support MAGTF maneuvers at the tactical and small-unit levels. Their small size, light weight, brief set-up time, and unique capabilities enable SUASs to be emplaced within any unit in the battlespace to provide near-real-time day/night airborne surveillance through full-motion video (FMV) and still image collection. They can be effectively employed in support of a battalion tactical air control party or company fire support team. As an organic air reconnaissance asset, SUASs can be rapidly deployed, usually require minimal transit time to their operating areas, and can therefore respond rapidly to a commander's tactical needs.

Three group 1 SUASs are organic to a variety of MAGTF units: the RQ-11B Raven DDL, RQ-12A Wasp All-Environment (AE), and RQ-20A Puma AE. The preponderance of SUAS assets are assigned to the ground combat element and do not have to be requested from the ACE. Some SUASs are assigned to the logistics combat element and the Marine wing support squadron. Small unmanned aircraft systems are employed by units at the battalion echelon and below, as well as by Marine special operations command companies and teams. They operate under the staff cognizance of the battalion air officer and are tasked by the S-3 in close coordination with the S-2.

The Raven B DDL, Wasp AE, and Puma AE provide complementary capabilities and share a common GCS, but each fills the need of differently sized units and operating environments. They provide an organic reconnaissance/surveillance capability for target acquisition and force protection, operating at a range of three to eight miles. There are typically four SUASs per battalion, or one per Marine special operations team.

Small unmanned aircraft systems can be launched from vehicles and small boats, providing a previously nonexistent airborne surveillance capability to mobile units (including foot mobile units) or units operating on the high seas or in the littorals, allowing a commander to cover significant geographic areas with airborne reconnaissance. All SUASs are fully autonomous with in-flight reprogramming capability. These systems are battery operated and use modular electro-optical-infrared (EO/IR) payloads with high-definition resolution to sufficiently identify the hostile intent of a man-size target.

The Wasp AE and Puma AE can operate under or through obscurants and low clouds that would preclude the use of other assets. They can also operate in rainfall of up to 1-inch per hour and can land in water, giving the commander significant collection and observation capability during poor weather. The Puma AE is capable of carrying additional payloads to include SIGINT/ electronic warfare, hostile forces tagging, tracking and locating, communications/data relay, and a 1064-nm laser pointer. The Wasp AE is capable of daytime clandestine surveillance due to its small size, delta-wing shape, and extremely low acoustic signature.

All three SUASs can be assembled and hand-launched by a single operator in 10 minutes; however, the Raven B DDL and Puma AE are optimized with two operators. Marine Corps SUAS operators are collateral duty personnel who assume one of two crew positions:

- *Vehicle Operator.* Responsible for flying the air vehicle using the hand controller as the man-to-machine interface.
- *Mission Operator.* Responsible for monitoring the SUAS mission. This includes launching the aircraft and monitoring flight using the reconnaissance, surveillance, and target acquisition (RSTA) laptop and software.

Small unmanned aircraft system operators will perform the duties of the vehicle operator and mission operator interchangeably. No qualification or certification distinction exists between the two crew positions. Although crew positions and responsibilities are the same for all three SUASs, operators must specifically train for each SUAS and be designated in writing by their commander as an operator for that particular SUAS. All crew members participate in mission planning, briefing, execution, and debriefing.

MARINE UNMANNED AERIAL VEHICLE SQUADRONS

Marine unmanned aerial vehicle squadrons support the MAGTF commander during expeditionary, joint, and combined operations by conducting EMS warfare, multisensor reconnaissance, and surveillance; supporting arms coordination and control; and destroying targets day or night and under all weather conditions.

Per the Marine Corps Task List, VMUs perform six core tasks: aviation operations from expeditionary shore-based sites, air reconnaissance, CAS, SCAR, aerial escort, and supporting arms control. Marine unmanned aerial vehicle squadrons also conduct aviation operations from expeditionary sea-based sites, armed reconnaissance, air interdiction, aviation support of tactical recovery of aircraft and personnel, and suppression of enemy air defenses, as well as coordinate electronic warfare capabilities within a combined arms framework.

Of the Marine Corps' four VMUs, three are active duty and one is reserve. A fifth VMU has been confirmed under Marine Corps total force structure but has yet to be activated. Table 2-1 provides more information on the Marine Corps' active VMUs.

Table 2-1. Marine Unmanned Aerial Vehicle Squadrons.

Squadron	Location	Assigned To	Supports
VMU-1	MCAGCC, Twentynine Palms, CA	3d MAW	I MEF
VMU-2	MCAS Cherry Point, NC	2d MAW	II MEF
VMU-3	MCAS Kaneohe Bay, HI	1st MAW	III MEF
VMU-4	MCB Camp Pendleton, CA	4th MAW	MARFORRES

Legend
MARFORRES—Marine Forces Reserve
MAW—Marine aircraft wing
MCAGCC—Marine Corps Air-Ground Combat Center
MEF—Marine expeditionary force
MCAS—Marine Corps air station
MCB—Marine Corps base

Each VMU is assigned two UASs, the RQ-7B Shadow and RQ-21A Blackjack, which are discussed in the following subparagraphs.

RQ-7B Shadow

The RQ-7B Shadow is a lightweight, rapidly deployable, short-range airborne system. An organic VMU asset, this system is operated by an aircrew of three Marines: an unmanned aircraft commander (UAC), air vehicle operator (AVO), and mission payload operator (MPO):

- The UAC is responsible for the overall conduct of the mission. Through leadership and supervision, the UAC ensures that mission planning complies with the air tasking order (ATO) and supported unit requirements. The UAC directs the UAS flight, conducts external coordination, and ensures proper integration of the UAS into the scheme of maneuver. The UAC is primarily responsible for communications and coordination during mission execution.
- The AVO is responsible for managing control inputs to the UAS for all phases of flight from launch and recovery, flight path, and navigation to the operation of any on-board systems related to flight functions.
- The MPO is responsible for the efficient and effective use of all aircraft sensors and/or payloads. The MPO manipulates the sensor, processes the data to be sent to the supported unit, and recommends approaches and tactics to employ sensors to the rest of the crew.

The aircrew may be augmented by an intelligence analyst (0231) or imagery analyst (0241), who are used interchangeably when supporting UAS operations, if required. Although analysts are not part of the aircrew, they are fundamental members of the support element and facilitate timely and accurate analysis of the information derived from UASs. These analysts are assigned to the VMU by table of organization and are responsible for developing timely and accurate mission-focused intelligence estimates. This entails conducting assessments, synthesizing information, and fusing new information with existing all-source intelligence.

An intelligence or imagery analyst is typically necessary when the RQ-7B Shadow is tasked to support intelligence, surveillance, and reconnaissance (ISR) in addition to air reconnaissance. The RQ-7B Shadow system consists of four aircraft; nine high mobility multipurpose wheeled vehicles (two with GCSs); and towed equipment that includes equipment trailers, generators, and launch and recovery equipment. The high mobility multipurpose wheeled vehicles serve to transport the personnel and GCS shelters, provide facilities for limited maintenance, and carry the four unmanned aircraft. The four aircraft are included as system subcomponents, each with combined EO/IR payloads. The EO/IR payload is capable of day/night operations with target surveillance out to 10 km and target recognition out to 7 km. This pneumatic rail-launched system can launch in crosswinds up to 20 knots and recover on short prepared runways of at least 710 feet using the tactical automated landing system. Additionally, the RQ-7B Shadow is augmented by a capability set IV tactical combat operations center (COC) that consists of multiple tents, network switches, and communications equipment.

RQ-21A Blackjack

The RQ-21A Blackjack is a small, flexible, and rugged expeditionary system capable of operating from austere land-based locations as well as from amphibious ships. It is ideally suited for supporting Marine expeditionary unit (MEU) operations both ashore and afloat. Each active VMU owns and operates nine RQ-21A Blackjack systems and can provide RQ-21A Blackjack detachments in operational support primarily to regiments, battalions, and MEUs. The RQ-21A Blackjack system consists of five unmanned aircraft; two GCSs; a launcher; a mechanical recovery system; transportation vehicles with trailers, tents, or shelters; spare parts; and support equipment. The system is scalable to the mission requirements of supported units and detachment personnel, and equipment can be task-organized according to specific mission requirements. RQ-21A Blackjack detachments can be employed in either general support or direct support roles and are designed to move and collocate with the supported unit. The RQ-21A Blackjack system can be self-mobile, using its organic vehicles and trailers to transport the entire system, including the launcher and recovery devices. The supported unit can opt to provide vehicles to move the system if sufficient motor transport assets are available. If required, all RQ-21A Blackjack system equipment and personnel can also be transported by CH-53 or KC-130 aircraft. The RQ-21A Blackjack can provide general support to maneuver units from regiments down to independent battalions.

The RQ-21A Blackjack is capable of providing day/night airborne reconnaissance, intelligence processing, target acquisition, and communications relay capability to the supported unit. The RQ-21A Blackjack is crewed by a UAC and UAS operator. The UAS operator performs both AVO and MPO functions. The aircrew may be supported with an intelligence or imagery analyst providing the supported unit an immediate intelligence estimate, preventing a delay caused by relying on another agency to transform the raw data into usable, actionable intelligence. Mission specifics such as the amount of air reconnaissance coverage per day and the type of sensors required will drive the task organization by the VMU and will dictate the personnel and equipment required to meet the mission.

An unmanned mission commander (UMC) may, as required, be assigned to a mission to instill unity of command over multiple UASs. Where unity of command must be identified for missions supported by two or more UACs simultaneously, one UAC must be assigned as the UMC. The UMC retains final authority for tactical employment of each UAS crew participating in the assigned mission.

The UMC is responsible for all phases of the assigned mission except those aspects of safety of flight related to the control of the unmanned aircraft and are within the prerogative of the UAC. The UMC may exercise command over a single or multiple UASs. The UMC shall be properly qualified and designated but need not be a winged aviator or commissioned officer. The UMC shall direct a coordinated plan of action and be responsible for effectiveness of the mission.

TASK ORGANIZATION OF MARINE UNMANNED AERIAL VEHICLE SQUADRON DETACHMENTS

A fully staffed and equipped VMU has sufficient personnel to operate three independent RQ-7B Shadow systems and nine RQ-21A Blackjack systems. Marine unmanned aerial vehicle squadrons task-organize to support the MAGTF based on operational requirements. The squadron commander is responsible for ensuring proper personnel and equipment task organization. Table 2-2 provides an initial point from which to plan the appropriate level of VMU support to the appropriate MAGTF.

Table 2-2. Marine Unmanned Aerial Vehicle Squadron Support to the MAGTFs.

Supported Unit	Supporting VMU Detachment
MEF	3 RQ-7B Shadow Detachments
	9 RQ-21A Blackjack Detachments
MEB	1 RQ-7B Shadow Detachment
	3 RQ-21A Blackjack Detachments
MEU	1+ RQ-21A Blackjack Detachment

Legend
MEB—Marine expeditionary brigade
MEF—Marine expeditionary force

These detachments are capable of providing direct or general support to units depending on the nature and duration of the mission. These support relationships are set by the MAGTF commander according to the tactical situation. The detachments may rely on the supported unit for administrative and support functions such as force protection, billeting, transportation, messing, communications, power generation, and vehicle maintenance if the requirements exceed those provided by the VMU detachment.

CHAPTER 3
PLANNING

PRINCIPLES FOR EFFECTIVE EMPLOYMENT

The versatility of UASs allows them to perform tasks within five of the six functions of Marine aviation and provide a significant contribution to the MAGTF during all phases of Marine Corps combat operations. Planning is essential to ensuring that UASs are properly and effectively integrated within the MAGTF commander's scheme of maneuver. This requires communication between MAGTF staff planners and UAS planners during the development of the MAGTF operation order. MAGTF staff planners must consider the tenets discussed in the following subparagraphs during operation order development.

Plan Early and Continuously

Persistent UAS coverage, a wide array of capabilities, and flexibility inevitably mean that some aspects of UAS operations will always be dynamic during execution. As soon as staff planners have reasonable certainty as to what organic and nonorganic UASs will be available to support the MAGTF, they must begin to plan to incorporate these capabilities. As operations draw nearer, planners must refine integration based on confirmation of available assets, payloads, and capabilities. Refinement must continue after the MAGTF commander signs the operation order to ensure the most efficient and effective use of the UASs.

Maximize Integration

To achieve its military objectives, the Marine Corps relies on the complementary employment of both manned and unmanned platforms, which often comprise the most effective aviation support solution. Limited quantities of assets and personnel require Marine Corps platforms to provide mutual support to achieve the greatest collective effect.

A significant advantage of the Marine Corps family of UASs is the organic support to the MAGTF from the tactical to the operational levels. Tactical-level commanders have organic SUASs that provide a wide variety of effects and capabilities and require little extra coordination outside the fire support coordinator and air officer. Should additional support or capabilities not inherent to organic SUAS assets be required, the appropriate request for support should be made. Requests for group 2 UASs and above should follow the standardized aviation tasking methodology for manned aircraft.

All support requests should reflect desired capabilities or effects based on current conditions vice a specific type of platform. Unmanned aircraft systems are high-demand, low-density assets; therefore, clarifying a support request by describing the desired result allows staff planners to fulfill requests more flexibly with a limited range of resources. Support requests that specify a type of aircraft or material solution may suffer delays due to the prioritization or limited availability of the specified asset, even if other assets are available that may satisfy the requestor's needs. If organic MAGTF UASs cannot provide the level of support or requested capabilities, further coordination through the ACE is required to request theater or strategic assets provided by other Services.

Supported units should consider all available assets and strive to achieve synergistic effects that maximize effectiveness. This requires a proper balance between sensor coordination, cross-cueing, digital interoperability, and mutual support, which are discussed in the following subparagraphs.

Sensor Coordination. Sensor coordination ensures that multiple sensors are not redundantly focused on a single point in the battlespace. If sensors are coordinated to focus on the same point, it is to exploit the benefit of using those sensors in concert. For example, during an air assault insertion, not all sensors need to observe and broadcast the actual insertion of forces by assault support aircraft. It may be more important for sensors to be distributed over the entire objective area and scan multiple avenues of approach for threats to the assault force vice concentrating on a single avenue and potentially alerting the enemy of the actual approach corridor's location.

Cross-Cueing. Cross-cueing occurs when the sensors from multiple platforms cooperate within an assigned objective area to expedite the location of assigned targets and hand them off to the appropriate assets. Given the capabilities and limitations of some sensors, search patterns of a large area can be a methodical and time-consuming endeavor. Other platforms may help reduce the time by locating targets and drawing a specific platform's sensors to such targets. For example, consider a situation in which two assets are searching a large area for armored vehicles. One asset is equipped with electro-optical sensors; the other is equipped with a ground moving target indicator sensor. The asset with a ground moving target indicator sensor may detect armor first and then provide a location to the other asset, allowing the other asset to place its electro-optical sensor directly on the target for high-definition surveillance.

Digital Interoperability. Digital interoperability through waveforms such as Link 16, Tactical Targeting Network Technology, and Adaptive Networking Wideband Waveform is key for successful cross-cueing and providing fused situational awareness during UAS employment. The digital sharing of UASs' precise position location information and sensor points of interest provides near-real-time geolocation information to all participants in the network, allowing for the effective cross-cueing of multiple sensors simultaneously and enhancing speed in delivering fires. Digital interoperability also allows SUASs to share sensor data such as lines of bearing for electronic signal geolocation across the family of UASs, which enhances the detection and rapid geolocation of threat emitters. Through digital interoperability, manned and unmanned aircraft are able to collaborate in real time without voice, exponentially increasing effectiveness across Marine aviation.

Mutual Support. Mutual support occurs when sensors cooperate in the same area to achieve a specific desired effect. For example, if two assets are observing two vehicles at a single location, both assets can maintain a track on both vehicles simultaneously. If the vehicles move in different directions, the two assets can each follow a separate vehicle to ensure the supported commander's desired effects are achieved. Digital interoperability is a key component in enabling electronic mutual support and is critical to the integration of manned and unmanned aircraft together in the battlespace.

Ensure Unity of Command

Units planning UAS support must maintain communication with their higher headquarters and subordinate units to facilitate unity of command. Unity of command between supported units ensures effective UAS employment during execution and provides many benefits. Ensuring unity of command entails reducing redundancy, establishing UAS priorities of support, and establishing handoff procedures.

Reducing Redundancy. If both a major subordinate element and a major subordinate command desire to observe the same objective area but have not properly communicated, they risk requesting UASs for the same mission. This unnecessarily congests the airspace and deprives other units of essential assets. With proper coordination, both units will be able to access the same UAS FMV feed.

Establishing UAS Priorities of Support. When a single UAS supports the requirements of multiple units within the same proximity, it is important that the higher headquarters clearly delineate priorities of support for UAS tasking. This ensures that retasking the UAS in flight maximizes its effectiveness and minimizes any negative impact to other units. Clearly defining priorities of support reduces the need for communication between UAS crews and supported units, streamlines guidance for diverting or maintaining tasking, and reduces task saturation.

Establishing Handoff Procedures. Clearly established and delineated UAS handoff procedures are critical. These procedures should include, at a minimum, a common communications medium, such as an assigned chat room or single-channel radio frequency. This ensures common situational awareness is shared between supported units and the supporting UAS. Handoffs are not limited to exchanges between units or between units and higher headquarters; they may also occur between different entities within the same unit (e.g., battalion S-2 to air officer or joint terminal attack controller [JTAC] to company). Handoff procedures must also specify control points and expected handover times for receiving units.

Coordinating and Integrating Airspace. Unmanned aircraft system airspace must be carefully planned to ensure the safe flight for all airspace users within the same objective area without being unduly restrictive to UASs. Supported units should conduct preflight coordination to ensure they understand the surveillance and coordinate generation, target identification, and target detection range capabilities of a particular UAS sensor, which may vary greatly from platform to platform. Integrating UASs requires the careful consideration of airspace coordinating measures (ACMs) and fire support coordination measures. Airspace coordination for Marine Corps UASs should emphasize integration with manned aviation vice segregation. Specific airspace planning methods will be discussed later in this chapter.

TACTICAL PLANNING CONSIDERATIONS

The availability of mission-essential planning information is key to successful UAS missions. Factors to consider include the items listed in table 3-1.

Table 3-1. Unmanned Aircraft System Planning Matrix.

Target Considerations	Area of Operations

Target description
Time on target
Target coordinates
  -Latitude/longitude
  -Grid
	Latitude/longitude
	  -Grid

Launch and Recovery Area	**Waypoints and Checkpoints**

Latitude/longitude
Grid
  -Outbound heading
  -Outbound altitude
	Latitude/longitude
	  -Assigned altitude
	  -Outbound heading

Special Airspace	**Holding Area**

Corridors/minimum risk routes
  -Entry point latitude/longitude
  -Entry point grid
  -Entry altitude
  -Transit heading(s)
  -Transit altitude
  -Exit altitude
  -Exit point latitude/longitude
  -Exit point grid
	Latitude/longitude
	Grid
	Altitude

Return Home Point	**Payload Type**

Latitude/longitude
  -Grid
  -En route altitude
Action upon arrival
  -Orbit altitude
  -Ditch
Lost communications routes
Lost communications hold times
	Electro-optical sensor
	Infrared sensor
	Communications relay package
	Laser pointer
	Laser designator
	Weapons
	Electronic warfare
	Others

Distance	**Administrative Considerations**
Control station to target and return	Are SOPs, LOAs, and MOUs current?
Frequency Considerations	**Communications Considerations**

UA control link
  -Uplink _____MHz
  -Downlink _____MHz
  -Separation from other agencies
Payload control link
  -Uplink: _____MHz
  -Downlink: _____MHz
	Controlling agency
	  -UHF
	  -VHF
	  -IRC window (e.g., mIRC)
	Supported unit
	  -UHF
	  -VHF
	  -High frequency

Table 3-1. Unmanned Aircraft System Planning Matrix. (Cont'd)

Maps	Execution
Are up-to-date maps available?	Brief time
Are these maps loaded into the system?	Launch time
Control measure overlays	Time over target
	Recovery time
	Total mission time
	Debrief time

Legend
MHz—megahertz
MOU—memorandum of understanding
LOA—letter of agreement
SOP—standing operating procedure
UA—unmanned aircraft

Unmanned aircraft flights must follow all approved planning, guidance, and procedures as prescribed in the ATO, airspace control order (ACO), and special instructions (SPINS). The ACO provides for separation of all types of aircraft—manned and unmanned, fixed- and rotary-wing—by defining altitude layers and geographic operating zones.

Small unmanned aircraft system operations will not appear as line number sorties on the ATO because they operate below the coordinating altitude. However, expected SUAS operating times, working areas, and other specifics shall be listed as footnotes in the ATO and updated in the SPINS. The following subparagraphs discuss considerations that should be taken into account when planning for UAS operations.

Transfer of Control
Mission planners should include the potential for contingencies that would require transferring control of the unmanned aircraft from the primary operator's GCS to another GCS, such as in hub-and-spoke operations, which will be discussed in greater detail in chapter 5. While transfer of control is inherent to hub-and-spoke tactics, it can also be accomplished whenever the operational situation dictates. Examples of such situations include one RQ-21A Blackjack detachment handing over an unmanned aircraft to another during an emergency or one GCS displacing with its supported unit and regaining control of an unmanned aircraft once relocated.

Duty Day
Commanders must take into account UAS crew fatigue to ensure units are sufficiently manned to accomplish desired missions. A commander will dictate the employment of personnel based on the combat situation. Due consideration must be given to address the risks involved with operating UASs in shared military or civil airspace and the condition of the UAS operators. Additionally, UASs present a different fatigue issue compared to manned aviation that affects crew quality, safety, and effectiveness. For example, UAS operators can experience "zoning out" from the lack of stimuli during extremely long-duration surveillance missions, which can negatively affect their recognition of critical details, communications, and decisionmaking ability. Generally, UAS crews should be rotated or replaced every 8 hours, waiverable by the commanding officer to 12 hours. Specific rest requirements and day limitations for UAS aircrew members are defined in the

OPNAV Instruction 3710.7 series publications. Additionally, intelligence and imagery analysts should be rotated with aircrew members to maintain their focus and attentiveness.

Emergency Planning

The typical sensory inputs that pilots experience in manned aircraft are absent when attempting control or recovery of unmanned aircraft experiencing system malfunctions. Unlike manned platforms, UAS crews are completely reliant on instrumentation transmitted through the system's data link for emergency input. A major consideration for all UAS operations is the potential to lose that data link. All DOD unmanned aircraft have planned or programmed lost-link profiles created by the operator before flight. The aircrew must ensure that these lost-link profiles are safe and consistent with all airspace requirements, follow ACO guidance, and deconflict with other airspace users.

Vulnerability

Combat operations have demonstrated that UASs can be susceptible to UAS countermeasures. Operational risk management procedures should be used during the mission-planning process to evaluate the threat environment and its impact on UAS operations. Unmanned aircraft systems are susceptible to interference from other systems operating in close proximity. All UAS components should be evaluated for susceptibilities and vulnerabilities, including the GCS, unmanned aircraft, payloads, and communications links. Unmanned aircraft system crews must maintain close liaison with the G-6 spectrum manager to understand potential GPS [Global Positioning System] outages and when communications and electromagnetic systems in theater may inadvertently affect UAS operations. The majority of problems pertaining to UAS communications links are caused by friendly interference.

Route Planning

Unmanned aircraft system missions flown by VMU detachments should be planned in coordination with the ACE's future plans and operations. This ensures effective integration with other ACE operations and allows timely inclusion of UAS missions into the ATO-planning process. Unmanned aircraft systems can typically use similar routing structures and airspace allocation methods as those used for manned aircraft. This includes the keypad system, which is a grid system established by the direct air support center (DASC) to facilitate procedural control of aircraft within the same airspace and control aircraft traversing between different points on the keypad.

Deceptive Routing

The routing of the unmanned aircraft can be used to deceive the enemy and cause him to expose himself to fires. Deliberately exposing unmanned aircraft to enemy observation can cause the enemy to make false assumptions on the intent of friendly forces, potentially influencing his actions and movements. The enemy may relocate or withdraw forces and materiel resources to defend against a perceived attack. Similarly, airspace managers must guard against using repetitive routes to the same locations. When an enemy becomes familiar with the flight pattern of an aircraft, that aircraft becomes easier to target.

When planning the route of an unmanned aircraft, as with that of any airborne asset, attention must be given to enemy air defenses. Unless the mission is to expose or draw out possible air defense sites, the aircraft should be routed around possible enemy air defenses to increase aircraft survivability. The RQ-21A Blackjack and RQ-7B Shadow typically operate at the heart of the antiaircraft artillery and man-portable air defense envelope, while group 1 SUASs are more vulnerable to enemy small-arms fire due to their lower operating altitudes and airspeeds.

Terminal Area Airspace Planning

Once in the terminal area of operations, UASs must be integrated into the airspace with other aviation assets. Modern UAS flight algorithms and flight control systems can reliably track unmanned aircraft location within a 10-digit coordinate and within ±30 feet vertically. Because of this precision, manned aviation platforms can safely be assigned altitudes with as little as 1,000-ft vertical separation from unmanned aircraft. However, UAS terminal area operational patterns should be separated from manned aircraft flight patterns to the maximum extent possible to avoid potential midair collisions.

TASKING

Marine Corps UASs are tasked in two different ways: units with organic UASs will task their systems per their commander's guidance and priorities and units requesting UAS support will follow the same tasking method for any air request. Once airborne, any UAS asset may be dynamically tasked or retasked.

Organic Direct Support Tasking

Organic direct support tasking generally applies to group 1 SUASs. Requests for support are internally staffed by the senior aviation representative or dedicated representative of the owning unit's command staff. Organic to the battalion level and below, SUAS employment is tasked by internal C2 processes established by their commander and small-unit leaders. Therefore, it is the commander's responsibility to properly allocate organic SUASs to conduct air reconnaissance or determine when other resources are better suited to accomplish the required task.

Aviation Tasking

Unmanned aircraft in groups 2 through 5 (including the RQ-21A Blackjack and RQ-7B Shadow) are tasked via the air tasking cycle. For detailed information on the joint air tasking cycle and Marine Corps air tasking cycle, see JP 3-30, *Command and Control of Joint Air Operations*, and MCWP 3-2. All requests for UASs within a unit are made via the commander's staffing process. All requests for air support—whether for operations, intelligence, communications, or other purposes—must be requested through the unit's appropriate staff officers. The staff officers who receive the request are responsible for the identification, prioritization, and target or mission unit selection based on the supported unit commander's objectives and concept of operations. Requests are submitted within the Marine Corps air tasking cycle via DD Form 1972, *Joint Tactical Air Strike Request*, or DD Form 1975, *Joint Tactical Air Reconnaissance/Surveillance Request*.

Specific theater requirements from the joint force commander (JFC) may supplement or require deviation from the following:

- During joint operations, MAGTF air assets typically support the MAGTF mission.
- The MAGTF commander will make sorties available to the JFC for tasking through the joint force air component commander (JFACC), providing air defense, long-range interdiction, and long-range reconnaissance.
- Sorties in excess of MAGTF direct support requirements will be provided to the JFC for tasking through the JFACC for the support of other components of the joint force or the joint force as a whole.
- Sorties provided for air defense, long-range interdiction, and long-range reconnaissance are not excess sorties and will be covered in the ATO.

For more information, see JP 1, *Doctrine for the Armed Forces of the United States*.

Dynamic Tasking

Dynamic tasking refers to the retasking of an airborne aviation asset following an immediate air support request. Marine air-ground task force UAS users must carefully draw the distinction between an asset being dynamically tasked or simply receiving new tasking from a supported unit. As discussed, unity of command is critical to ensuring that priorities and handoff procedures are established so that general support tasking is effective and information flow is complementary to operations.

Dynamic tasking of an airborne UAS requires the immediate approval of a mission with a higher priority than the mission for which the UAS was originally allocated and assigned. The decision to dynamically task a UAS will reside with a C2 agency assigned the authority to make such decisions. As such, dynamic tasking may only be authorized by the appropriate commander.

It is critical that MAGTF planners and UAS end users understand the relationship of apportionment and allocation of air assets within the MAGTF. Unmanned aircraft systems will not be used to drive task allotment for UAS assets. Just as other MAGTF air assets are tasked, UAS apportionment will be determined by the MAGTF commander's priorities through the commander's staff. This apportionment will reflect the degree of tasking that will be allocated and allotted for all incoming requests for UAS support.

Electronic Warfare Tasking

The tasking of UAS electronic warfare payloads is similar to dynamic tasking but uses members of the MAGTF cyberspace and electronic warfare coordination cell (CEWCC) to develop conceptual and functional plans. Such an organizational construct allows for supporting and supported roles to shift as required in the planning and execution of EMSO and shaping operations in support of the MAGTF commander. Electromagnetic spectrum operations are defined as the coordinated efforts of electronic warfare and electromagnetic spectrum management operations to exploit, attack, protect, and manage the electromagnetic operational environment. Unmanned aircraft system electronic warfare payloads will deliver intended nonkinetic effects and/or provide electronic warfare support collection as part of a system-of-systems approach. However, the CEWCC is not expected to execute VMU operations in their totality but merely coordinate and facilitate the delivery of applicable effects in cyberspace, SIGINT collections, and/or information operations synchronized via EMSO. First and foremost, CEWCC is a coordination and synchronization element of the G-3 or S-3 intended to prevent any MAGTF entity from planning and/or tasking electronic warfare payload operations in isolation.

The CEWCC lines of effort (LOEs) are depicted in figure 3-1. These LOEs have been established via DOD architecture framework products designed to provide the battle rhythm of typical G-2/S-2, G-3/S-3, and G-6/S-6 activities in support of electromagnetic spectrum operations. Though the planning and execution of EMSO are deliberate in their intent, technologies associated with current and future nodes require a very dynamic C2 environment. Electromagnetic spectrum operations should replicate the established ideals of centralized command and decentralized control.

From these LOEs, two critical EMS coordinating documents and one coordinating matrix of all activities emerge, directly impacting the tasking of UAS payloads. Using these tools, CEWCC members are able to articulate EMS and electromagnetic operational environment

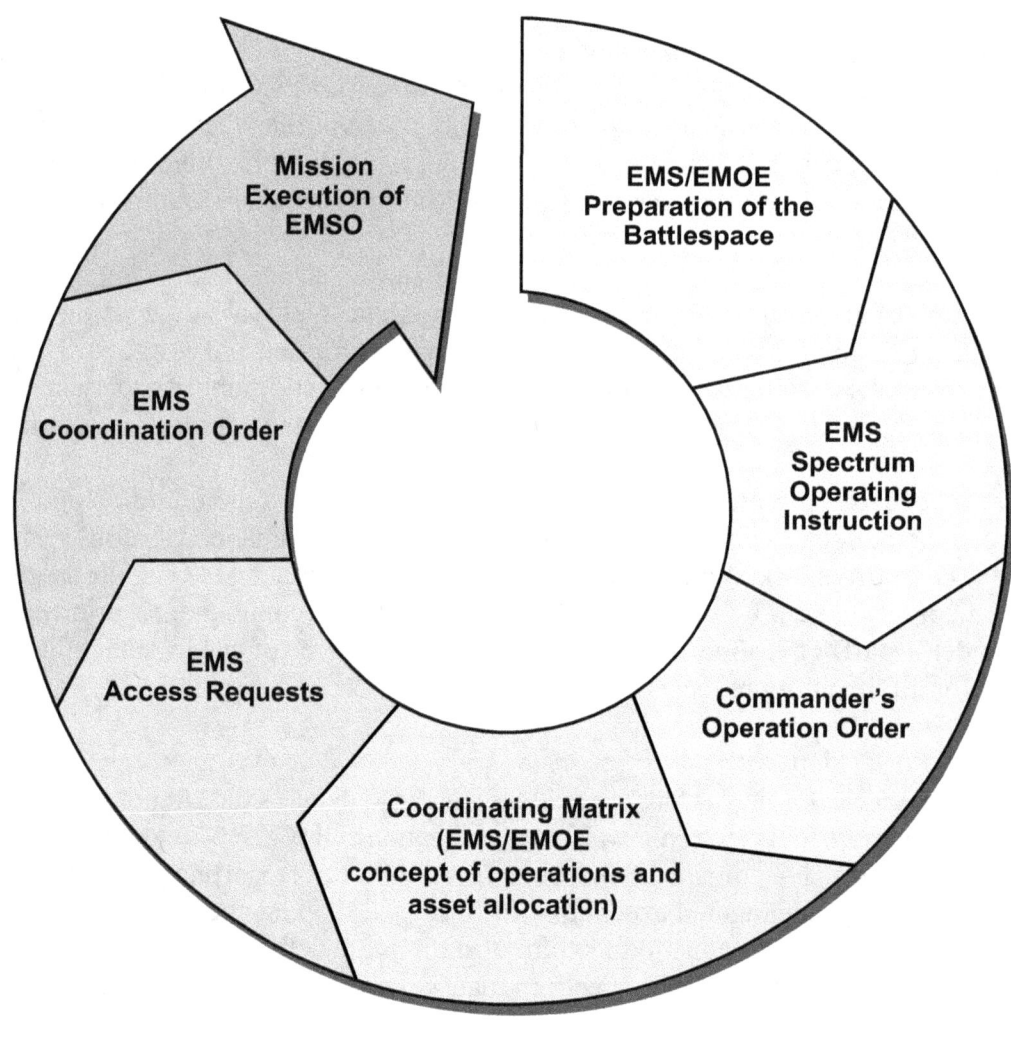

LEGEND
EMOE   electromagnetic operational environment

Figure 3-1. Cyberspace and Electronic Warfare Coordination Cell Lines of Effort.

requirements to the other operational planning teams within the MAGTF. For example, targets will emerge from the coordinating matrix derived from the CEWCC or from established MAGTF targeting processes.

AIRSPACE COORDINATION

The established principles of airspace management used in manned flight operations typically apply to UASs. Effective airspace control reduces the risk of fratricide, enhances air defense, and permits flexibility. With the introduction of advanced systems and sensors, modern unmanned aircraft fly in airspace with precisely defined limits. As such, airspace planners should make every effort to integrate UASs into the complex airspace, vice isolating them from manned aviation. Digital interoperability of UASs, such as the inclusion of UAS metadata into Link 16, creates significant advantages for airspace planners and greatly increases safety of flight. Mitigation of airspace user risk is provided through ACMs disseminated in the airspace control plan, ACO, and SPINS of an air tasking order. Use of these documents is essential for the planning and integration of manned and unmanned aircraft operations.

The RQ-7B Shadow typically operates between the altitudes of 3,000 and 7,000 feet above ground level (AGL), straddling both rotary- and fixed-wing traffic areas. Although technically designated a group 3 UAS, the RQ-7B Shadow maintains the physical ability to operate at altitudes up to 15,000 mean sea level. The RQ-7B Shadow is equipped with a transponder and controlled by both positive and procedural control methods. Both methods of control require two-way communications with air traffic controllers in terminal areas and with other controlling agencies, such as the DASC or the US Air Force's air support operations center in the operational working areas.

The RQ-21A Blackjack is equipped with a transponder and typically operates between the altitudes of 3,000 and 5,000 feet AGL. The RQ-21A Blackjack's operating times and working altitudes will be clearly delineated on the ATO and ACO to facilitate coordination with manned aircraft operating in the same airspace.

Small unmanned aircraft systems typically operate at altitudes below 1,200 feet AGL and do not carry a transponder. These altitudes do not usually conflict with fixed-wing aircraft but may require coordination with rotary-wing traffic. Airspace requirements are coordinated between SUAS operators, the company-level forward air controller/JTAC, and the battalion S-3/air officer. Operational areas of SUASs are contained within boundary lines of ground units that own the SUAS assets. Airspace coordinating measures and other coordinating instructions such as operating areas, times, and altitudes are transmitted from battalion air officers to the DASC for immediate ACO or SPINS updates. The DASC and battalion air officer provide general SUAS location information to pilots of manned aircraft, especially pilots of low-flying, rotary-winged and tilt-rotor aircraft.

CONSIDERATIONS FOR EFFECTIVE OPERATIONS

The following subparagraphs discuss several other important considerations unique to UAS operations.

Ground Support Planning

Ground support planning supports all nonflight UAS planning necessary to support and sustain the employment of the VMU. This requires a survey of the potential operating site for suitability to operate, launch, and recover unmanned aircraft and physical obstacles to datalinks and other communications nodes. Consideration must be given to locating the GCS, with its C2 and payload datalinks, away from any radio frequency emitters that would interfere with the communications links between the unmanned aircraft and its control station. The RQ-7B Shadow requires larger operational sites than the RQ-21A Blackjack due to its need for runways and larger approach and departure corridors.

Threats

Unmanned aircraft losses to hostile fire are caused primarily by small arms and antiair artillery weapons. Any number of tactical, strategic, and technological factors will continue to threaten unmanned aircraft in the future. The unmanned aircraft itself, however, is not the only vulnerable component within a UAS. The survivability of UASs depends on measures taken to reduce vulnerability of the total system, to include the GCSs, air vehicles, and Marines who operate and maintain the systems. Both active and passive threat techniques can degrade or deny the ability of a UAS to fulfill its intended mission. In the case of SUASs, the operator will be vulnerable to the same fires and effects as the frontline unit being supported (i.e., small arms, direct fires, and indirect fires).

Airspace

The military airspace control authority is responsible for the safe operation of UASs and integration of the systems into military airspace. This requires continuous communication and detailed planning through the ATO and ACO cycles. In operations where UASs operate from a host nation, the Service or functional component JFACC is responsible for airspace management and integration issues for all UASs operating in the combined force. In a major combat operation, the JFC will typically control the airspace and UAS operators will follow the JFC's guidance found in the theater airspace control plan, as outlined in JP 3-52.

As discussed, SUASs are not required to appear on the ATO and will typically be tactically controlled by a qualified SUAS operator from the ground unit that owns the UAS. Outside the MAGTF area of operations, SUAS operations are not controlled because they are flown beneath the coordination altitude. Airspace coordinating measures specific to SUASs may be immediately established through an appropriate air control agency. However, if the capability exists, inclusion of the SUAS ACMs on the ACO will benefit all airspace users by providing the most advanced notice. Additional SUAS notes may also be included in the SPINS.

Weather

Weather has always been a consideration in aviation operations and is especially important to consider when planning UAS operations. Unmanned aircraft system planners and operators must carefully consider the expected meteorological effects on UAS employment. Most unmanned aircraft or their payloads can be negatively affected by precipitation, wind, and temperature. Aircraft that weigh less and operate at slower airspeeds are more affected by strong winds. Small propellers with high RPM [revolutions per minute] are affected by debris and rain. Electro-optical-infrared sensors have limited capabilities for penetrating dust, fog, and cloud layers.

The RQ-12A Wasp AE and RQ-20A Puma AE are all-weather platforms. They can fly in rain (of up to 1-inch per hour) and light snow and can land in water (fresh or salt water). Because they are weatherized, they can also fly through visible moisture (e.g., clouds, haze, fog, mist) to and from an objective area. However, no Marine Corps UASs are currently authorized to fly in icing conditions.

Communications

Unmanned aircraft system operations are highly dependent on multiple communications paths. These two-way communications paths, or data links, transmit aircraft control input and payload control signals. Most UAS data links rely on LOS communications in the L, S, and C frequency bands and can be either analog or digital signals. The current Marine Corps SUASs operate in the digital L band. The primary C2 and telemetry data links for the RQ-7B Shadow are S band with ultrahigh frequency (UHF) band secondary, while the video downlink is in the C band. Both RQ-7B Shadow links will transition to a Ku tactical common data link. The RQ-21A Blackjack will initially be operated in digital L, S, or C bands. Table 3-2 lists typical frequency ranges for various UAS C2 bands.

Table 3-2. Unmanned Aircraft System Command and Control Frequency Bands.

Band	Typical UAS Frequency Range
Ku	14.4–14.83/15.15–15.35 GHz
C	4.4–4.9/5.25–5.85 GHz
S	2.2–2.5 GHz
L	1.71–1.85 GHz
UHF	400–470 MHz
	1625–1725 MHz (SUAS/M1 RF unit/OCONUS)
	1755–1850 MHz (SUAS/M2 RF unit/CONUS)

Legend
CONUS—continental United States
GHz—gigahertz
MHz—megahertz
OCONUS—outside the continental United States
RF—radio frequency

Unmanned aircraft systems are limited by their ability to operate only in a specific frequency range. Therefore, units desiring to employ UASs must coordinate with the MAGTF G-6/S-6 frequency managers, who, in coordination with the theater spectrum manager, will allocate specific frequencies to be used. Many communications systems such as GPSs, other SATCOM systems, and even local UHF systems are susceptible to electromagnetic interference (EMI).

Planners must consider other emitters in the local area of the GCS and the unmanned aircraft to avoid EMI, including hostile EMI, EMI from civilian operations, and unintentional friendly EMI. Radio frequency waves that travel closer to the Earth's surface, such as those emitted by terrestrial data transmission systems (e.g., TRC-170), pose the greatest EMI threat to UASs. Electromagnetic interference is also prevalent in the vicinities of high-powered radars especially aboard ships.

To mitigate inadvertent friendly EMI, intentional hostile intercept, and interference of the uplink and downlink, UAS data links should be both frequency hopping as well as secure. The uplink controls the activities of the unmanned aircraft and the payload and requires sufficient security to ensure only authorized agents can access its control mechanisms. The return downlink transmits critical data—such as system health and status information—from the platform payload to the operator or analyst in the GCS, which must be delivered without compromise.

If operating in congested areas of known EMI, the unit frequency manager may be able to offer mitigating techniques or, if feasible, suggest alternate frequencies. Since frequency issues often need to be coordinated with civilian or host nation frequency management agencies, this coordination process can take more than six months. Consequently, early planning for utilization of UASs in such areas is essential to successful UAS operations.

Communications Among the Unmanned Aircraft System Crew, Supported Unit, and Airspace C2 Agencies. The communications link among the UAS crew, supported unit, and airspace C2 agencies is as equally important as the communications link between the GCS and the unmanned aircraft. Ideally, the UAS crew should maintain direct communication—either face-to-face or electronically—with both the supported unit's operations cell (watch officer, air officer, and/or fires officer) and intelligence section. Synergy between operations and intelligence through direct communication enables enhanced operational effectiveness, especially in time-sensitive targeting situations.

Communications between the UAS crew and supported units can take place in a variety of forms: telephone, Voice over Internet Protocol, Internet relay chat (IRC), SATCOM systems, and doctrinal very high frequency (VHF)/UHF radio nets. When LOS and range restrictions prohibit VHF/UHF nets, a UAS with an on-board communications relay package can enable direct communications between the UAS crew and the supported unit.

Remote Video Terminals. Supported units can access FMV directly from the unmanned aircraft with an RVT, which is often the most practical means of receiving video and telemetry information for tactical users such as platoon and company commanders, forward air controllers, JTACs, and air officers. The RVT is typically a ruggedized laptop with an antenna and software that enables data processing and direct viewing of sensor imagery and telemetry information. Typically, the RVT has limited range and can receive video from within approximately 15 km of the unmanned aircraft. Some have much larger directional antennas that can receive video from beyond 45 km. The RQ-7B Shadow is equipped with four RVTs called One System remote video transceivers. The VMU can loan a One System remote video transceiver to supported units such as a regimental COC to receive video and telemetry reception directly from an RQ-7B Shadow (and certain other UASs) from greater distances. However, the Marine Corps' primary RVT is the VideoScout system, the fastest, most direct means of distribution. Fielded to ground maneuver units, tactical air control parties, and battalion air officers, VideoScout can view video with metadata on analog or digital L, S, C, and Ku frequency bands. Other units or headquarters equipped with a VideoScout and within range of the unmanned aircraft can also receive the same video imagery. This multilayer distribution capability ensures multiple paths for UAS imagery and reduces delays for high-priority users.

In situations where a more remote unit or agency desires video and telemetry data, the MAGTF G-6 must develop a communications architecture that will facilitate the transmission of large volumes of FMV/telemetry data. Marine Corps UASs can provide a STANAG-compliant, interoperable data stream that interfaces or plugs into networks created by the MAGTF G-6. The plug-in would be applied to a system integral to the COC. The COC would then provide the interface to the DCGS-Marine Corps for distribution of intelligence products from the GCS and intelligence analyst. All MAGTF units connected to the DCGS-Marine Corps will then have access to the video/telemetry data provided by the UAS, though with increased levels of imagery latency and video compression.

Radio Links and Nets. Table 3-3, on page 3-15, identifies and describes several doctrinal communications nets and data links used in UAS operations. The communications plans of VMUs should have a certain level of redundancy to ensure uninterrupted command and control of the entire UAS through spectrum diversity (high frequency, VHF, and UHF), single-channel radios, voice over switching network, or other data networks. Additionally, planning should begin early as frequency spectrum requests can take exceedingly long times (up to 90 days for satellite link frequencies).

Internet Relay Chat. In addition to the supported units, UAS data is often shared across the battlefield and up and down the chain of command to enhance situational awareness beyond the immediate user level. Internet relay chat functions and features have become a primary communications means between the system operators and other agencies involved in UAS missions. Internet relay chat has also become a key element in the transmission of information for building situational awareness rapidly and historical archiving of information.

Latency. The term latency can be used in different ways when discussing UASs, each with a number of considerations. One form of latency is the time between the UAS crew's control input reaching the unmanned aircraft, the necessary action being taken, and the aircrew receiving the appropriate return signal. If the time lag in this sequence is too long, the aircrew may make multiple inputs to the system before their effects are actually seen. These problems are usually taken into account by the design engineers during development, but crews should also be aware of them.

A second, more prevalent type of latency is the time lag between an event and the moment the image of the event is transmitted on a video screen to the UAS aircrew and the supported unit. Time lag or latency differences between the UAS aircrew's picture and the supported unit's picture should be understood to avoid confusion. Latency between the actual event and the time the UAS crew and supported unit see that event should be measured in milliseconds, vice seconds, as this is the most critical user set. For this reason, VMU crews can be employed in direct support and be embedded with the unit. Placing the GCS in, or adjacent to, the unit's operations center would render the time lag negligible. As UAS video feed may also be disseminated through other tactical data networks, often to a higher headquarters, significant latency (up to several seconds) may occur. Higher headquarters in receipt of this delayed video should be aware that their tactical picture might be several seconds behind actions being taken by tactical commanders using this same video. This issue often presents itself during weapons engagement decisions, and its effects should be clearly understood and considered during planning.

Table 3-3. Radio Nets for Unmanned Aircraft System Operations.

Net Name	Frequency	Purpose
TAD Net	VHF/UHF	Used primarily for the terminal control of CAS missions and for procedural and positive control of aircraft in FAC/JTAC airspace. The UAC/UMC may receive air control from the FAC/JTAC through the TAD net.
TATC Net	VHF/UHF	Provides a means for the Marine TACC/TADC, TAOC, CEWCC, MATC detachment, and DASC to exercise control of all tactical and itinerant aircraft, including UA. Airspace for the UAS should be coordinated on the TATC network or via IRC (e.g., mIRC) to the ATC or DASC.
UAS Command Net	VHF/UHF	Used by the UAC to coordinate UA activities on the airfield. If the LRS is located at an extended distance from a control station, it may be necessary to establish this net via HF radio. Whenever possible, a telephone wire system should be installed as the primary communications means between the UMC and other mission-essential activities.
Landing Force Intelligence Net	HF/VHF/UHF-SATCOM	Provides a current situational information exchange with the MAGTF SARC. This net is used by the pilot to communicate with the SARC. Whenever possible, wire is the primary communications means among these stations.
Helicopter Direction Net	HF/VHF/UHF	Used by the UMC for close coordination between the UA mission commander and helicopters.
Naval Gunfire Spot Net	HF	Used by the UMC to assist the naval surface fires support ships to adjust fires support and provide target damage assessment.
Fire Support Coordination Net	HF/VHF-FM/UHF	Used by the UMC to coordinate or adjust supporting arms fire through the supported fire support coordination center or artillery unit headquarters.
Conduct of Fire Net	VHF-FM	Used by the UMC when adjusting artillery missions directly with the artillery battery or battalion.
Landing Force Reconnaissance Net	HF/VHF/UHF-SATCOM	Provides for coordination of the reconnaissance effort within the MAGTF. This net is an alternate communications means between the UMC and the reconnaissance unit to pass critical information when the doctrinal intelligence net is unavailable.
Landing Force Tactical or GCE Tactical Net	HF/UHF	Issued to pass FLASH precedence traffic when other means are not available. It may also aid the GCE commander in maneuver control. *Note*: Per MCRP 3-25B, *Multi-Service Brevity Codes*, "FLASH (system)" means "Clear the net immediately, critical information to follow."

Legend
ATC—air traffic control
FAC—forward air controller
FM—frequency modulation
GCE—ground combat element
HF—high frequency
MATC—Marine air traffic control
MEDEVAC—medical evacuation

SARC—surveillance and reconnaissance center
TACC—tactical air command center
TAD—tactical air direction
TADC—tactical air direction center
TAOC— tactical air operations center
TATC—tactical air traffic control
UA—unmanned aircraft

Contingencies

Lost Links. Loss of communications with the unmanned aircraft is an emergency condition. Unlike manned aircraft crews, UAS crews are completely reliant on instrumentation transmitted through the system's data link for emergency input. All DOD unmanned aircraft have planned or programmed lost-link profiles created by the operator before flight. Operators must ensure that these lost-link profiles are safe and consistent with all airspace requirements in accordance with the ACO and other airspace documents governing MAGTF-assigned airspace.

When the UAS senses a significant delay or loss of the command uplink, it will automatically enter into a return home mode of flight, flying a preapproved route and altitude toward a predetermined home site. During this emergency, the UAS crew will attempt to reestablish communications with the unmanned aircraft. If contact is reestablished, the aircrew will decide whether to terminate the mission and return to base to preserve the asset or, based on the tactical situation, continue the mission as planned. At the return home site, the unmanned aircraft will perform the programmed flight recovery maneuver unless communications have been restored and the AVO commands otherwise. To relocate a lost unmanned aircraft, consideration should be given to the use of identification, friend or foe systems and airspace control radars.

In-Flight Emergencies. During planning, sufficient attention must be given to the possibility of in-flight emergencies such as lost links, as discussed above, or engine malfunctions. Obstacle-free flight paths, minimum-risk routes, lame duck procedures, and other air management tools must be included. The UAS crew will execute the emergency procedures, notify the appropriate air control agency, and coordinate any changes to the route of flight due to the emergency. The use of a preplanned ditch site should be considered during UAS operations. The ditch site shall be selected based on its potential to minimize damage to the unmanned aircraft, ease its recovery, and prevent risk of endangerment to personnel or civilians.

CHAPTER 4
OPERATIONS

OPERATIONAL ROLES

Marine Corps UASs are designed to focus on tactical employment in support of the MAGTF. However, just as there is overlap in the levels of war, the Marine Corps family of UASs has overlap in its capabilities. There are situations in which a UAS supporting a tactical commander may have operational or even strategic implications. Nonetheless, UASs employed by Marines are primarily tactical assets. Marine unmanned aerial vehicle squadron detachments possess an organic intelligence analysis capability to expedite the process by which a commander gains understanding of the MAGTF's tactical environment.

Unmanned aircraft systems provide the MAGTF with useful information about the area of operations and warn of existing and emerging threats by remaining on station for longer periods than manned aircraft. Due to changing mission requirements and the need for the entire enterprise to share a common tactical picture or pass information, nodes must be established throughout the MAGTF battlespace. An unmanned aircraft system provides information throughout the MAGTF via common display platforms located, at a minimum, within the UAS GCS, G-2/S-2, G-3/S-3, and G-6/S-6. As a result, UASs provide airborne reconnaissance and surveillance and rapid flow of information that MAGTF analysts can quickly transform into real-time intelligence, which then becomes actionable intelligence for the MAGTF commander.

In amphibious operations, UASs may assist the advanced force commander—and subsequently the commander, amphibious task force and the commander, landing force—with accurate information to be developed into timely intelligence. However, several considerations must be taken into account, including—

- Distance of amphibious objective area from the UAS launch point.
- Ability of friendly forces to receive data over extended distances from shore.
- Enemy antiaircraft capabilities.
- Ability to hide friendly intentions.
- Weather in operating area.

Unmanned aircraft systems give the commander the ability to develop real-time amphibious objective area intelligence prior to an amphibious assault. The data from the UAS should be able to give imagery of the beach area including the craft landing zones, natural and manmade obstructions, enemy command and control with imagery and radio frequency sensors, other hazards to the amphibious force, and deep strike targets. Unmanned aircraft systems can be employed to assist in the observation, coordination, delivery, and adjustment of fires in the amphibious objective area.

Special operations require robust covert UAS capabilities. Unmanned aircraft can operate over an objective area for minutes, hours, or days ahead of the arrival of special operations forces and provide continuous reconnaissance and valuable intelligence to operators on the ground.

CONCEPT OF OPERATIONS AND TACTICS

Lessons learned from combat experience in Operations OIF and OEF have significantly influenced UAS tactics, techniques, and procedures as well as the organization of the VMU squadron itself. Ground units are expanding their use of organic UASs, and the VMU now provides multiple detachments to a MAGTF commander. The end state for the Marine Corps family of UASs is to provide a capable UAS or a VMU UAS detachment to MAGTFs of any size.

Surveillance and Reconnaissance for Maneuver Units

Primary airborne surveillance and reconnaissance for maneuver units will be provided by their organic SUASs. These assets, distributed down to the company/team level, are used to provide immediate, mobile, persistent FMV; still imagery; and limited SIGINT/electronic warfare capability to frontline units in direct contact with enemy forces. Because SUASs are relatively low in cost and do not contain sensitive/classified payloads, they are considered expendable (but not disposable) and are designed for use across the spectrum of conflict and through the range of military operations, to include high-threat environments. During combat operations in Iraq and Afghanistan, SUASs were proven to be extremely durable, reliable, and difficult for the enemy to detect or counter. When heavy obscurants, low cloud ceilings, or visible moisture and precipitation are present, SUASs may be the only unmanned aircraft available to the maneuver element.

Movement Operations (Launch, Displace, and Recover)

Fires and maneuver have long been established as a tenet in Marine Corps tactics. The ability to retain expeditionary mobility is built into the VMU squadron and determines the types of UASs procured for the force. Unmanned aircraft system tactics can be similarly employed to retain fluidity in the battlespace using displacement. Unmanned aircraft system units and personnel can employ movement tactics by launching an aircraft, passing control to another GCS (or other detachment for control), and then displacing to another site to reassume control and prepare for recovery of its unmanned aircraft. This tactic provides a means to operate with maneuver forces during a major advance, as seen in the opening weeks of combat in Operation OIF. This freedom of movement also permits the UAS detachment from being fixed in one place and subsequently targeted while executing a UAS mission.

Single-Site Operations

Unmanned aircraft system operations can be established and flown from a single location. The benefits of this type of employment include increased command and control, reliable communications nodes, and predictable logistics and site support functions. A drawback of this type of beddown site is that the area of influence and range of action for the UAS unit are limited.

Currently, UAS range and LOS restrictions limit the extent to which the UAS can operate and influence operations. Additionally, units established in one place for an extended period will often make continual improvements to their site location that can significantly add support requirements beyond that required for the original beddown configuration. Considerations for this type of employment include force protection concerns and the requirements for hardening and improving the unit's position.

BATTLESPACE COORDINATION

Time-Sensitive Targets

Marine unmanned aerial vehicle squadron UAS aircrews with support element intelligence and imagery analysts can rapidly assimilate and fuse information into intelligence, giving them the ability to identify an individual or vehicle as a time-sensitive target (TST), which can be critical to the support of TST missions. Unmanned aircraft system aircrews should follow established procedures for supporting joint TST (as described in MCRP 3-16D, *Multi-Service Tactics, Techniques, and Procedures for Dynamic Targeting*). Aircrews should identify when a TST has been found and determine whether they are responsible for the emerging target. They should coordinate directly with the supported unit to highlight the TST to cognizant authorities. Aircrews may also be called upon to act as a supporting commander for the TST mission. Time-sensitive target situations may require UASs to support CAS, SCAR, airborne interdiction, other joint fires missions, and priority intelligence requirements. In the TST role, UASs are routed, controlled, coordinated, or integrated in the same manner as manned fixed- and rotary-wing aircraft as outlined in joint doctrine. Unmanned aircraft systems often have the advantage of long endurance and persistence such that greater time is afforded to track and follow a TST, making it less likely to evade detection.

Transfer of Control During Mission Execution

An inherent advantage of UASs and their relatively long endurance is the ability to be diverted from one mission to another. If a UAS is retasked to support a higher priority mission, the new supported commander must be knowledgeable of established UAS C2 procedures to alleviate the necessity for impromptu instruction in unmanned aviation operations. Immediate retasking of a UAS, based on the commander's guidance, will be coordinated through the DASC. Two-way communications between the VMU crew and the new supported unit must be established immediately using radio, chat, Voice over Internet Protocol, or other relay means. While the unmanned aircraft is en route to the new task, the supported unit should pass relevant, abbreviated, mission-type information, such as the situation, mission, execution, administrative and logistic requirements, and command and signal instructions to the UAS crew via any means possible.

RECONNAISSANCE INFORMATION AND INTELLIGENCE MANAGEMENT

The UAS is primarily employed in the conduct of air reconnaissance supporting current operations and the production of intelligence for the commander. Marines operating UASs should become thoroughly familiar with the concepts of information and intelligence found in MCWP 2-1, *Intelligence Operations*. Information can be defined as raw data, facts, or instruction presented in any form.

Information and Intelligence

There is a clear and important distinction between information and intelligence. Intelligence is not a mass of unfocused data or even a collection of related facts. In actuality, providing every piece of data without meaning can increase uncertainty by overloading the commander with incomplete, contradictory, or irrelevant information.

Figure 4-1 provides a framework to distinguish between various classes of information. To be considered intelligence, raw data must be placed in context to provide an accurate and meaningful image of the hostile situation. Intelligence is developed by analyzing and synthesizing data and information to produce knowledge about the threat and environment. The commander combines this intelligence with knowledge of the friendly situation and employs experience, judgment, and intuition to understand the situation. The commander then applies this understanding when making decisions. Unmanned aircraft system aircrews and VMU-organic intelligence and imagery analysts interact closely with the supported unit's intelligence cells. This two-way flow of information between the VMU and the supported unit's intelligence specialists often enables rapid development of intelligence based on the real-time FMV, coupled with other relevant information fused by the team of intelligence experts.

The following guidelines are especially important to the UAS aircrew so that they can effect timely, quality intelligence vice an overabundance of meaningless imagery or featureless FMV:

- Use the supported commanders' information requirements to define the information flow.
- Tailor information to the commander's tactical needs and filter unnecessary information.
- Use multiple sources of information.

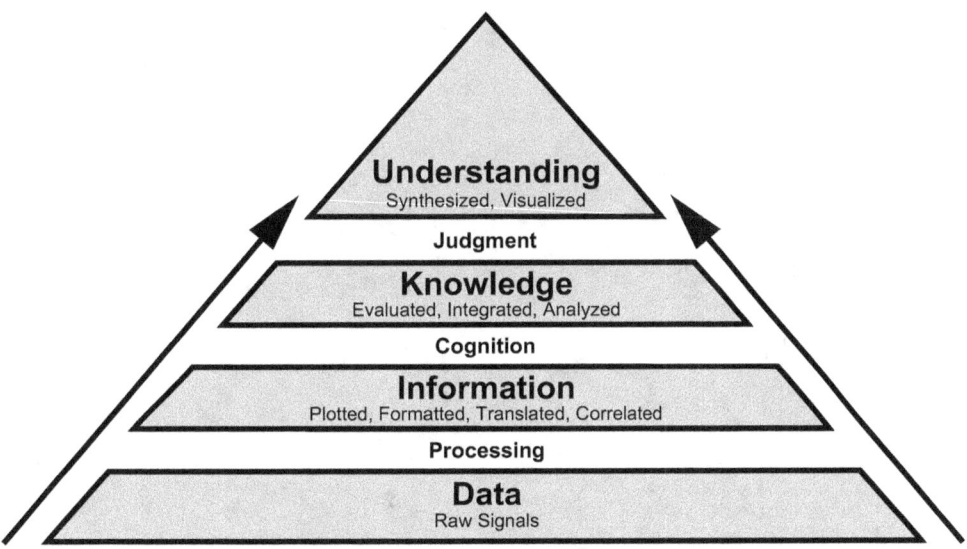

Figure 4-1. The Information Hierarchy.

- Deliver the information on time.
- Disseminate accurate and relevant information.
- Create flexible and redundant procedures and plans.
- Protect information through a vigorous security program. If the enemy can intercept an unencrypted video or metadata stream, the element of surprise will be lost and the enemy can alter his plans to counter friendly action or employ deception. A caveat to this security requirement is to avoid over-classifying information that will preclude its timely use by those who need the information.

The Intelligence Cycle and the Tasking, Processing and Exploitation, and Dissemination Process

Doctrinally, Marine Corps intelligence is developed through a six-step (see fig. 4-2) intelligence cycle:

- Planning and direction of intelligence efforts is where pertinent information requirements are identified and means are determined to meet those requirements.
- Collection is the gathering of information and intelligence to satisfy the identified requirements and consists of the activities of organic, attached, and supporting intelligence collection assets to gather new data and deliver it to appropriate processing or production entities.

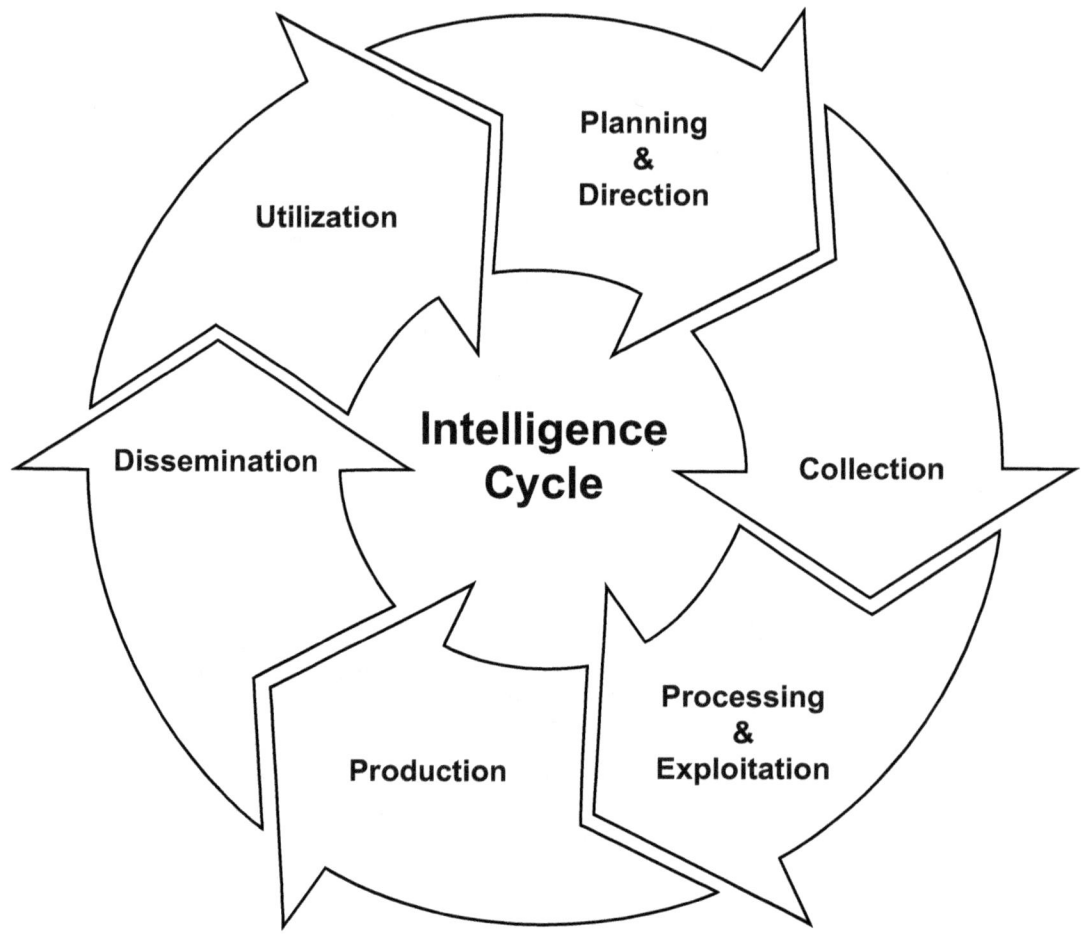

Figure 4-2. The Intelligence Cycle.

- Processing and exploitation is the conversion of collected data into information suitable for the production of intelligence.
- Production is the evaluation, interpretation, integration, analysis, and synthesis of all information relevant to a particular information requirement into a usable, actionable intelligence product.
- Dissemination is the timely conveyance of intelligence to users in an appropriate format.
- Utilization of intelligence occurs in the decisionmaking process of the commander.

The UAS community speaks of this process in a slightly modified fashion and combines some of the steps to accelerate the process and provide intelligence to decisionmakers as quickly as possible. A UAS aircrew and support crew must be able to disseminate combat information, processed intelligence, and fire support data rapidly to the appropriate users. Tasking, processing and exploitation, and dissemination are the abbreviated intelligence process steps for UASs. Figure 4-3, on page 4-7, shows the relationship between the intelligence community's six-step intelligence cycle process and the UAS tasking, processing and exploitation, and dissemination process:

- Tasking is the identification, coordination, and positioning of assets and/or resources to satisfy collection objectives. Tasking of Marine Corps UASs is a collaborative effort between the operations and intelligence sections; however, the formal requesting and tasking process is done through operational channels. Collection is a result of the tasking of assets to gather the information.
- Processing and exploitation is the conversion of collected information into forms suitable for the production of intelligence. Marine Corps UASs are designed to expedite the conversion of raw sensor data into products that can be readily utilized without significant manipulation of the imagery, video, or other sensor data. Intelligence and imagery analysts are embedded as part of the VMU and perform initial processing and intelligence production, greatly expediting the production step. Generally, imagery is screened by VMU intelligence or imagery analysts for information of immediate tactical value in accordance with the intelligence collection plan and reporting criteria stipulated by the intelligence support coordinator or the supported unit's intelligence officer. Intelligence and imagery analysts also provide the added benefit of providing formal positive identification of specific targets during certain situations (i.e., when the rules of engagement dictate the need of an imagery analyst for positive identification of a TST). Their estimate can be evaluated and analyzed in further detail by other analysts after this initial look.
- Dissemination is the delivery of intelligence to users in a suitable form and the application of the actionable intelligence information to the supported unit commander. Due to the presence of organic intelligence and imagery analysts, this dissemination of actionable intelligence is nearly instantaneous within the VMU.

Imagery Intelligence
Per MCWP 2-21, *Imagery Intelligence*, imagery is the representation of objects reproduced electronically or by optical means on film, electronic display devices, or other media. Intelligence requirements such as imagery intelligence can form the basis of UAS operational tasking for supporting ISR or target acquisition missions.

Imagery intelligence is a function performed by the G-2/S-2 that involves imagery analysis and integration with other intelligence activities to produce all-source intelligence products. Generally,

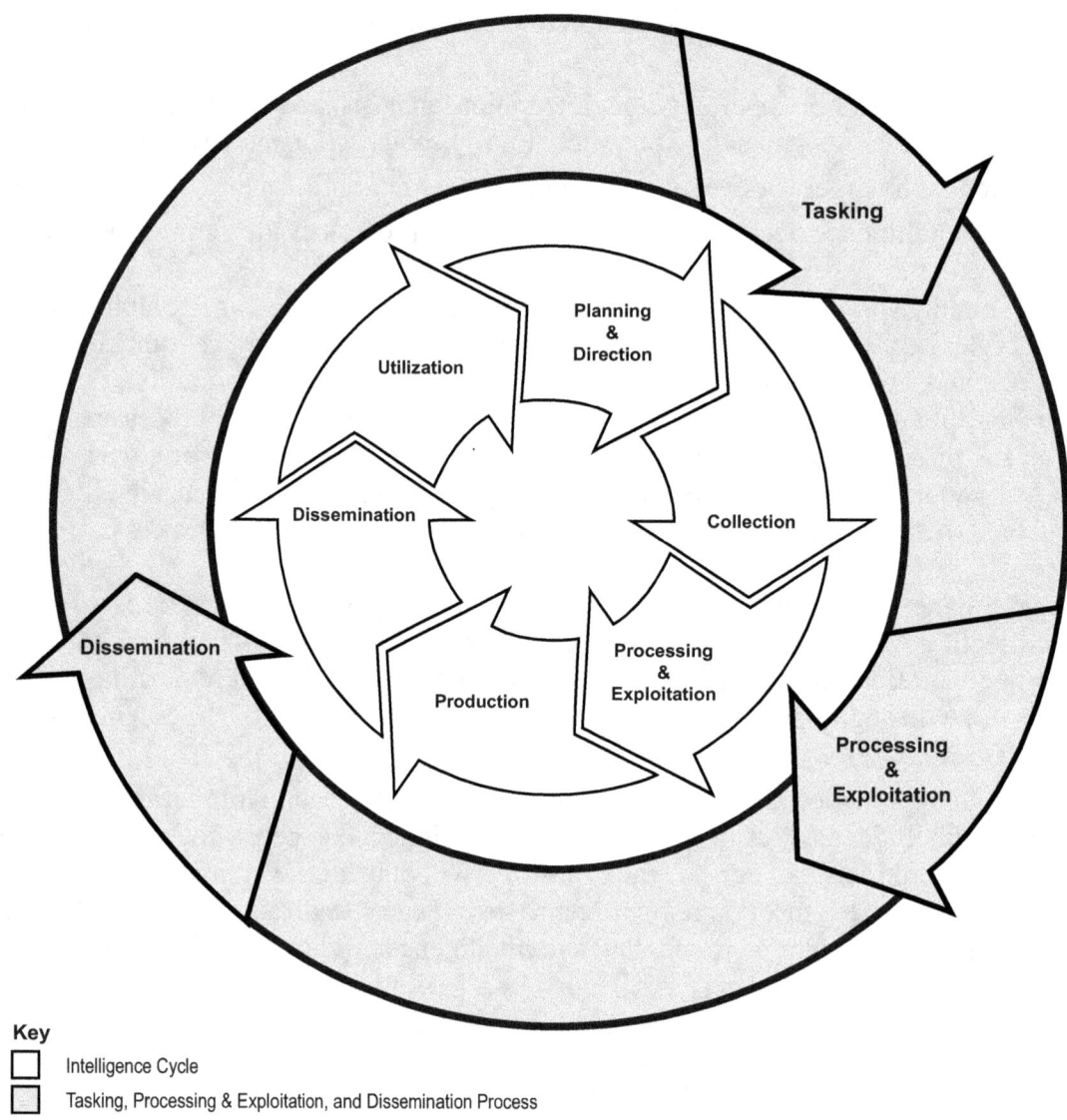

Key
☐ Intelligence Cycle
▨ Tasking, Processing & Exploitation, and Dissemination Process

**Figure 4-3. Comparison of the Intelligence Cycle
and the Tasking, Processing and Exploitation, and Dissemination Process.**

it is better to employ imagery collection resources against point targets, vice in a wide-area search mode. Effective integration with other intelligence operations can cue imagery collectors to key targets, narrowing the general search area and more rapidly producing useful intelligence. The need for a detailed target deck with an understanding of the mission's intent and clear collection objectives cannot be overemphasized.

Full-Motion Video. The most effective use to date of UASs has, by far, come from the use of FMV. The real-time view of enemy actions or friendly events contributes more to the commander's situational awareness than any other system in the commander's inventory, and as such, the demand for UASs with FMV capability has increased exponentially. The need for more FMV is often described as the need for more ISR, and UASs are mistakenly labeled as ISR platforms. Unmanned aircraft systems are air reconnaissance assets, capable of providing airborne reconnaissance and surveillance via FMV and other resources. Describing UAS FMV activities as ISR is thus incorrect, as FMV provides much more than ISR, and ISR is much more than FMV.

Unmanned aircraft system FMV provides battlespace awareness for a supported unit in a generic sense. Real-time FMV of the enemy situation can provide the commander a bird's eye view of the current situation and can be helpful in coordinating activities and events during current operations. This type of battlespace awareness video works best when provided directly to a supported unit's COC with little degradation of video quality or excessive latency. This use of video without intelligence analysis is often considered RSTA. Using RSTA to support a specific operation can be a very effective use of FMV. One example would be to use an RQ-7B Shadow or RQ-21A Blackjack to perform prelanding surveillance of a landing zone prior to a helicopter-borne assault.

Reconnaissance Imagery. The nature of intelligence requirements will dictate the type of imagery collection. Four types of imagery collection are—

- Area reconnaissance imagery collection.
- Point reconnaissance imagery targets.
- Route reconnaissance imagery.
- Strip search reconnaissance imagery.

IMAGERY STORAGE AND ARCHIVING

Unmanned aircraft system imagery is often stored locally by the VMU either directly on the system's memory or on additional data storage devices. The VMU typically does not store this information longer than three days, but with proper coordination, storage could be for up to 30 days. However, the long-term FMV/imagery storage requirement is the responsibility of the MAGTF G-2/S-2 and not the VMU.

ELECTRONIC WARFARE OPERATIONS WITH APPROPRIATE PAYLOADS

When considering airborne electronic warfare planning and execution, the most significant aspect is employment time. Traditionally, manned aviation operations are generally much shorter in duration and conducted at much higher speeds than ground operations. The inclusion of UASs with EMSO capabilities, such as a software-reprogrammable payload that can provide network connectivity, can also be reprogrammed to conduct an electronic attack. The targeting cycle requirements for electronic fires necessitate timely and detailed intelligence reporting. Due to an airborne receiver's enhanced LOS in the battlespace and the myriad of information users within the MAGTF, aviation electronic warfare support of the EMS kill chain may require a more extensive signals targeting database and a more detailed plan than is required for electronic warfare payloads operating on other host platforms.

Additionally, airborne electronic warfare support activities are usually conducted in general support of the MAGTF or the joint task force. However, the *Concept of Operations for Marine Air-Ground Task Force Electronic Warfare*, promulgated June 2011, describes the evolution of these concepts as focusing more on electronic warfare support capabilities down to company-level tactics, primarily with the use of UASs.

Airborne electronic warfare planning in support of EMSO must not only consider the host platform in the UAS but also the functionality provided by the payload (cyberintelligence, SIGINT, electronic warfare, or information operations) (see fig. 4-4 on page 4-10). Planners must also consider conceptual ideas including cooperative payloads operating in coordination against an adversarial command and control using a myriad of functionalities to complete kill chains, vice single nodes attempting to neutralize multiple systems. For example, SUASs are able to operate with a higher level of confidence due to reduced enemy detection, while larger UASs provide increased functional capacity in the form of payload size, weight, and power. Alignment considerations must also be factored based on the supported functionality and the characteristics of the victim system.

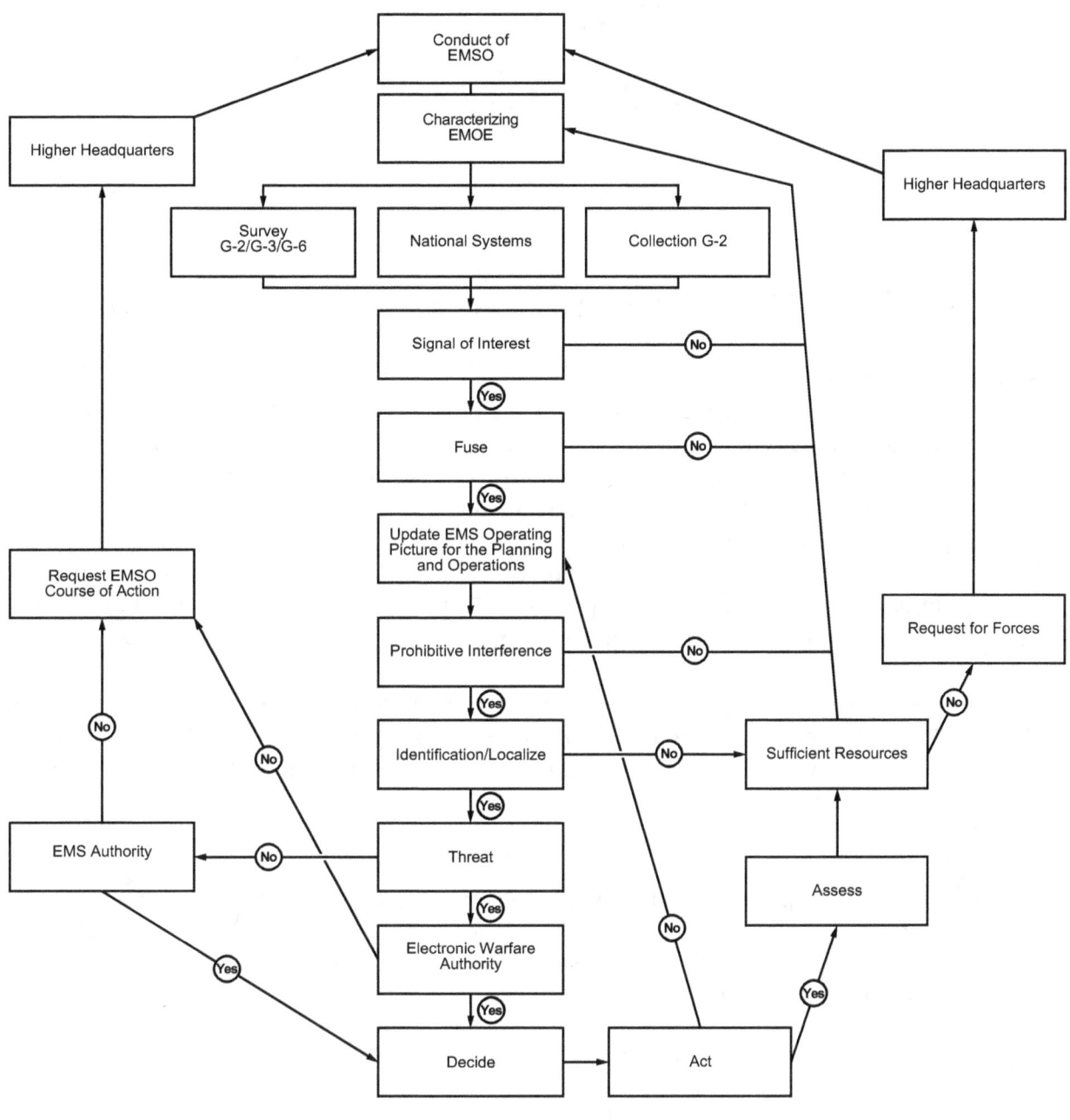

LEGEND
EMOE   electromagnetic operational environment

Figure 4-4. Decision Algorithm for Electromagnetic Spectrum Kill Chain.

CHAPTER 5
EMPLOYMENT

EMPLOYMENT CONCEPTS AND CONSIDERATIONS

Transportation Requirements

Both the RQ-7B Shadow and RQ-21A Blackjack are equipped with sufficient rolling stock to support independent system movement. Detachments that are prohibited from bringing their own organic motor transport assets due to footprint limitations, such as on a MEU, will be dependent on the supported unit for transportation of the detachment's equipment during employment. This should be agreed to and planned for prior to detaching to the supported unit. In the event a full VMU is employed as part of a Marine expeditionary brigade- or Marine expeditionary force-sized MAGTF, external motor transportation support from MAGTF units may be required to provide mobility for additional VMU personnel and equipment.

In the ship-to-shore movement phase of an amphibious operation, the full table of equipment for a VMU may require shipboard embarkation of its organic rolling stock to move the entire unit ashore. Once ashore, a VMU UAS detachment possesses sufficient rolling stock to maneuver with other MAGTF ground elements.

Supply Support

The MAGTF ACE, through the Marine aviation logistics squadrons, provides aviation supply support to the VMU's aviation assets. The naval aviation supply and maintenance system provides spares, repair parts, support and test equipment, and technical assistance. It also ensures that additional stocks are available through routine replenishment procedures. Supply support for a VMU's nonaviation requirements is provided with the existing Marine Corps system for provisioning and supplies. The Marine Corps logistics bases and the supported commander share supply responsibility for ground supply items. For the first three years, VMU UASs are often materially supported through contract maintenance programs as in the case of the RQ-21A Blackjack, until an organic maintenance program can be developed. Contract maintenance programs are obligated to provide operational spares, pack-up kits for extended training, and any pack-up kits for operational deployment. The use of contract maintenance, if required in combat, will require special planning as contractors are generally not permitted in direct combat situations. Contract maintenance is usually only conducted in secure, permanent operating bases and not remote, on-the-move locations.

Engineer Support

When a suitable site for UAS operations cannot be located, engineer support may be required to construct a site. For example, the RQ-7B Shadow using the tactical automated landing system requires a minimum landing area that is approximately 75 ft by 2,800 ft for climb-out and approach corridors. However, runway length of the RQ-7B Shadow is dependent on density altitude, which is pressure altitude corrected for ambient temperature. The runway length of 2,800 ft is the required length at sea level. At a density altitude of 10,500 ft, the RQ-7B Shadow would require approximately 3,200 ft of runway to clear the arresting net. The RQ-21A Blackjack is not dependent on runways and requires launch and recovery areas much smaller than the RQ-7B Shadow. The RQ-21A Blackjack is capable of launch and recovery from an approximately 50-m by 50-m area with a normal departure and recovery path free of obstacles. The primary support unit tasked with providing this engineering support to the VMUs is the Marine wing support squadron. If available, paved runways, improved roads (asphalt or concrete), and unimproved roads (hard dirt) may be used for takeoff and landing operations, in which case engineering support will not be required.

Power Generation
Unmanned aircraft system operations require a significant amount of electrical power and power distribution. Marine unmanned aerial vehicle squadrons have a sufficient number of mobile generators to provide self-sustaining electrical power to all its detachments. RQ-21A Blackjack detachments will have limited power generation capability and may rely on the supported unit for electrical power, as well as their heating, ventilation, and cooling needs.

EMPLOYMENT CONSIDERATIONS

Naval Tactics, Techniques, and Procedures 3-22.3-VMU, *Combat Aircraft Fundamentals VMU*, is the source document for tactical employment planning and standardized tactics, techniques, and procedures for Marine Corps UASs. This paragraph is intended to provide commanders and staffs with sufficient information to make general planning considerations for employing UASs with the rest of the MAGTF. While this paragraph does not apply to any specific UAS or unmanned aircraft group category, it refers generally to larger systems that rely on LOS unmanned aircraft control.

Operating Sites
Operating sites are the basic building blocks of UAS employment planning. The two types of UAS operating sites are the LRS, commonly referred to as the hub, and a split site, commonly referred to as a spoke. The LRS is a location in which maintenance, flight operations, and launch and recovery are conducted. The LRS may include a runway, depending on the types of systems being operated from that location. A split site is a location from which only in-flight operations can be conducted. Unmanned aircraft systems will be launched from and recovered at the LRS and handed off to the split site for tactical mission execution. A split site is not always required but may enhance the effectiveness of operations if used appropriately. A split site should be considered when the MAGTF requires—

- Extended UAS LOS control range.
- More streamlined UAS crew coordination with the supported unit.
- A UAS to overcome the effects of terrain on communications.

The terms "split site" and "LRS" are distinct from the terms "mission control element" and "launch and recovery element." The mission control element and launch and recovery element refer to specific equipment that performs a specific function at a given location. Split site and LRS refer to a specific function performed at a given location but do not have specifically associated equipment. The LRS, for example, means the same thing whether an RQ-7B Shadow, an RQ-21A Blackjack, a combination of the two, or other system is located there, even though the site will function differently based upon the equipment. These flexible terms allow MAGTF planners and UAS aircrews to employ systems while seamlessly integrating with the rest of the MAGTF. The VMU headquarters will typically be located at the hub. While mission planning will occur at both the hub and spoke, the location containing the VMU headquarters will typically be responsible to the ACE for operations conducted at all operating sites. Coordination between the hub and spoke is crucial during these dislocated operations.

Employment Configurations

Employment configurations are standard site configurations for individual UASs designed to simplify planning for physical system ground emplacement within the MAGTF's battlespace. Employment configurations define how the VMU postures to support tactical operations. Certain types of employment configurations may be well suited to complement certain types of MAGTF operations, but no employment configuration is specifically intended to support a specific type of MAGTF operation. Employment configurations do not necessarily directly correlate to a VMU's mobility or agility. A VMU is not restricted to a single employment configuration and may fluidly change employment configurations as necessary to support the MAGTF scheme of maneuver. When doing so, time to transition, UAS coverage, and external logistic and force protection support must be considered. The two types of employment configurations are centralized operations and distributed operations, which are discussed in the following subparagraphs.

Centralized Operations. When a VMU executes centralized operations, it conducts all operations from a single site. This configuration is ideally suited for providing general support to a MAGTF. This configuration maximizes manpower so that the supporting VMU is capable of providing the maximum amount of on-station support with the fewest number of crews. It also reduces VMU logistical and force protection requirements. However, this configuration also restricts the LOS operating range of the UAS and requires the greatest amount of communications support to disseminate products to and enable communications with supported units.

Distributed Operations. Distributed operations are executed by the VMU from one or more LRSs and one or more split sites. When using this employment configuration, the expectation is that supported MAGTF operations will require both the LRS and split site to conduct flight operations. This employment configuration is typically used when the MAGTF commander requires a VMU to simultaneously provide general support to the MAGTF and direct support to a specific element of the MAGTF. This configuration enables the VMU to support multiple MAGTF requirements and benefit from all the capabilities of a split site. However, this configuration also increases manpower requirements while reducing sortie numbers and on-station time. In centralized operations, one crew flies a single UAS; in distributed operations, multiple crews may be required to fly a single aircraft due to handoffs between the hub and spoke. Greater distances between the LRS and the objective area may further reduce on-station time due to transit time to and from the objective area.

Control Station Transfer

A control station transfer, or handoff, is a procedure by which one GCS transfers control of an unmanned aircraft to another GCS in flight. The most common reasons a UAS crew might execute a control station transfer include the following:

- To extend the LOS communications range to the unmanned aircraft.
- To seamlessly pass control from one to crew to another (especially when those crews are in geographically distinct locations).
- To troubleshoot when one GCS encounters maintenance issues.

> *Note:* Ground control stations for the RQ-7B Shadow and RQ-21A Blackjack are not interchangeable.

MARINE UNMANNED AERIAL VEHICLE SQUADRON MISSION EXECUTION

Flight Brief

The UAC will organize a flight brief that includes the UAS aircrew and intelligence, maintenance, and S-6 representatives. Briefs provide specific information in accordance with the VMU's standing operating procedures. Whenever possible, representatives from the supported units should attend flight briefs to describe UAS tasking and operational requirements. See the individual system OPNAVINST 3710.7, *Naval Air Training and Operating Procedures Standardization General Flight and Operating Instructions*, or pocket checklist and *Naval Tactics, Techniques, and Procedures 3-22.3-VMU, Combat Aircraft Fundamentals VMU.* for specific briefing guides.

Launch/Takeoff

The VMU or detachment maintenance personnel will prepare the unmanned aircraft for launch as the flight crew performs functional checks to ensure systems perform in accordance with OPNAVINST 3710.7. The UAS aircrew, in close coordination with a maintenance or safety observer, must follow the approved airfield or launch site procedures before and during launch and recovery of the UAS. A vertical or pneumatic launch takeoff requires no runway. However, a relatively flat and clear area must be available for a safe, obstruction-free launch. For example, the 375-lb RQ-7B Shadow requires at least 75 ft by 2,800 ft of obstruction-free area to allow the unmanned aircraft sufficient airspace to launch and climb out.

Recovery

The UAS aircrew will coordinate with the local air traffic control agencies (approach control and/or tower) for terminal area arrival and supervise the recovery operation to include navigation to the recovery site. The aircrew will monitor the UAS flight performance and perform unmanned aircraft recovery procedures in accordance with procedures while preparing the payload for landing. The crew chief can act as an outside safety observer for both launch and recovery operations.

> *Note:* During both launch and recovery operations, the UAS aircrew shall be in direct communications with the airspace control agency—usually the DASC or tower if at an airfield and the primary flight control tower if on a ship—and should have an observer outside the GCS or COC in order to facilitate direct observation of the UAS in the terminal area.

INTEGRATION WITH JOINT OR COMBINED FORCES

History illustrates that US forces traditionally operated as joint task forces and as members of a coalition in almost every modern military campaign. All US Services employ UASs, as do many foreign military forces. It is expected that future US military operations will consist of joint US forces or a combined force with coalition members. When conducting expeditionary operations, it is likely that US forces will be working with multiple coalition partners or with a single host nation. Unmanned aircraft systems designed for STANAG compliance can assist in meeting standards set by host nation officials for UAS operations in their sovereign airspace. The following key considerations must be taken into account when operating with coalition partners or a host nation:

- *Technology Interoperability.* When UASs are shared, planners must address potential difficulties such as security issues and incompatible hardware/software as early as possible in the planning process. Examples include making RVTs capable of receiving imagery from coalition UASs or providing US RVTs to coalition partners to allow them to receive video from US UASs.
- *Airspace Management.* As discussed, integrating UASs into joint/combined airspace amplifies an already complex challenge. All coalition UASs, regardless of nation of origin, should be held to the same standards, policies, and procedures as established by the host nation or airspace control authority. Additionally, when working with coalition UASs, it is critical to establish workable identification, friend or foe procedures.
- *Spectrum Management.* Spectrum conflicts were one of the leading causes of coalition unmanned aircraft mission cancellations in Operation OEF. Spectrum use requires detailed coordination with joint and coalition partners prior to operations.

FUTURE EMPLOYMENT

Unmanned aircraft system technologies are developing and maturing at a pace that far exceeds normal technical and doctrinal publication cycles. Unmanned aircraft system crew and planners should maintain an awareness of current operational practices and payload technologies. Future technologies such as beyond-line-of-sight unmanned aircraft, enhanced EO/IR devices, electronic warfare and SIGINT payloads, and weapons will likely be incorporated into the Marine Corps' assets well ahead of the next update of this publication. When possible, the Deputy Commandant for Combat Development and Integration will provide the appropriate changes to keep pace with these rapidly evolving technologies.

GLOSSARY

Section I. Acronyms and Abbreviations

AAW .... antiair warfare
ACE .... aviation combat element
ACM .... airspace coordinating measures
ACO ....airspace control order
AE ....all-environment
AGL ....above ground level
ATO .... air tasking order
AVO .... air vehicle operator

C2 ....command and control
CAS .... close air support
CEWCC .... cyberspace and electronic warfare coordination cell
COC .... combat operations center

DASC .... direct air support center
DCGS .... distributed common ground system
DDL ....digital data link
DOD .... Department of Defense

EMI ....electromagnetic interference
EMS .... electromagnetic spectrum
EMSO ....electromagnetic spectrum operations
EO/IR ....electro-optical-infrared

FMV .... full-motion video
ft ....feet

G-2 ....assistant chief of staff, intelligence
G-3 ....assistant chief of staff, operations
G-6 .... assistant chief of staff for communications
GCS .... ground control station

IRC .... Internet relay chat
ISR ....intelligence, surveillance, and reconnaissance

JFACC ....joint force air component commander
JFC ....joint force commander
JP ....joint publication
JTAC ....joint terminal attack controller

km .... kilometer

lb ....pound
LOE... line of effort
LOS .... line of sight
LRS ....launch and recovery site

m .... meter
MAGTF ....Marine air-ground task force
MAW .... Marine aircraft wing
MCRP ....Marine Corps reference publication
MCWP ....Marine Corps warfighting publication
MEU..Marine expeditionary unit
MPO .... mission payload operator

NATO .... North Atlantic Treaty Organization
nm ....nanometer

OEF .... Operation Enduring Freedom
OIF ....Operation Iraqi Freedom

RPV..remotely piloted vehicle
RSTA ....reconnaissance, surveillance, and target acquisition
RVT .... remote video terminal

S-2.. intelligence staff officer
S-3... operations officer
S-6.. communications system officer
SATCOM...satellite communications
SCAR...strike coordination and reconnaissance
SIGINT ....signals intelligence
SPINS..special instructions
STANAG .... NATO standardization agreement
SUAS ....small unmanned aircraft system

TST ....time-sensitive target

UAC ....unmanned aircraft commander
UAS .... unmanned aircraft system
UAV..unmanned aircraft vehicle
UHF .... ultrahigh frequency
UMC ....unmanned mission commander
US .... United States

VHF .... .very high frequency
VMU .... Marine unmanned aerial vehicle squadron

Section II. Terms and Definitions

air control—1. The authority to affect the maneuver of aircraft. 2. The authority to direct the physical maneuver of aircraft in flight or to direct an aircraft or surface-to-air weapon unit to engage a specific target. The elements of air control are air control agency, air controller, airspace control, operational control, positive control, procedural control, radar control, and terminal control. (MCRP 5-12C)

air control agency—An organization possessing the capability to exercise air control. (MCRP 5-12C)

air defense—Defensive measures designed to destroy attacking enemy aircraft or missiles in the atmosphere, or to nullify or reduce the effectiveness of such attack. Also called **AD**. (JP 1-02)

air direction—1. The guidance and supervision that a commander employs to focus his resources on mission accomplishment. 2. The authority to regulate the employment of air resources (aircraft and surface-to-air weapon units) to maintain a balance between their availability and the priorities assigned for their usage. Air direction occurs as a sequence of the air apportionment, air allocation, tasking, and fragmentary order development. (MCRP 5-12C)

air reconnaissance—2. The acquisition of information by employing visual observation and/or sensors in air vehicles. Air reconnaissance is one of the six Marine aviation functions. (MCRP 5-12C, part 2 of a 3-part definition)

airspace control authority—The commander designated to assume overall responsibility for the operation of the airspace control system in the airspace control area. Also called **ACA**. (JP 1-02)

airspace control order—An order implementing the airspace control plan that provides the details of the approved requests for airspace coordinating measures. It is published either as part of the air tasking order or as a separate document. Also called **ACO**. (JP 1-02)

airspace control plan—The document approved by the joint force commander that provides specific planning guidance and procedures for the airspace control system for the joint force operational area. Also called **ACP**. (JP 1-02)

airspace coordinating measures—Measures employed to facilitate the efficient use of airspace to accomplish missions and simultaneously provide safeguards for friendly forces. Also called **ACMs**.

amphibious objective area—A geographical area (delineated for command and control purposes in the initiating directive) within which is located the objective(s) to be secured by the amphibious force. This area must be of sufficient size to ensure accomplishment of the amphibious force's mission and must provide sufficient area for conducting necessary sea, air, and land operations. Also called **AOA**. (JP 1-02)

close air support—Air action by fixed- and rotary-wing aircraft against hostile targets that are in close proximity to friendly forces and that require detailed integration of each air mission with the fire and movement of those forces. Also called **CAS**. (JP 1-02)

combat operations center—The primary operational agency required to control the tactical operations of a command that employs ground and aviation combat, combat support, and logistics combat elements or portions thereof. The combat operations center continually monitors, records, and supervises operations in the name of the commander and includes the necessary personnel and communications to do the same. Also called **COC**. (MCRP 5-12C)

combined arms—1. The full integration of combat arms in such a way that to counteract one, the enemy must become more vulnerable to another. 2. The tactics, techniques, and procedures employed by a force to integrate firepower and mobility to produce a desired effect upon the enemy. (MCRP 5-12C)

command—1. The authority that a commander in the armed forces lawfully exercises over subordinates by virtue of rank or assignment. Also called **CMD**. (JP 1-02, part 1 of a 3-part definition)

command and control—The exercise of authority and direction by a properly designated commander over assigned and attached forces in the accomplishment of the mission. (JP 1-02) The means by which a commander recognizes what needs to be done and sees to it that appropriate actions are taken. Command and control is one of the six warfighting functions. Also called **C2**. (MCRP 5-12C)

control—1. Authority that may be less than full command exercised by a commander over part of the activities of subordinate or other organizations. (JP 1-02, part 1 of a 4-part definition) A tactical task to maintain physical influence by occupation or range of weapon systems over the activities or access in a defined area. (MCRP 5-12C)

control of aircraft and missiles—The coordinated employment of facilities, equipment, communications, procedures, and personnel that allows the aviation combat element commander to plan, direct, and control the efforts of the aviation combat element to support the accomplishment of the Marine air-ground task force mission. Control of aircraft and missiles is one of the six functions of Marine aviation. (MCRP 5-12C)

coordinating altitude—An airspace coordinating measure that uses altitude to separate users and as the transition between different airspace coordinating entities. Also called **CA**. (JP 1-02)

coordination—The action necessary to ensure adequately integrated relationships between separate organizations located in the same area. Coordination may include such matters as fire support, emergency defense measures, area intelligence, and other situations in which coordination is considered necessary. (MCRP 5-12C)

deep air support—Air action against enemy targets at such a distance from friendly forces that detailed integration of each mission with fire and movement of friendly forces is not required. Deep air support missions are flown on either side of the fire support coordination line; the lack of a requirement for close coordination with the fire and movement of friendly forces is the qualifying factor. Also called **DAS**. (MCWP 3-25)

direct air support center—The principal air control agency of the US Marine air command and control system responsible for the direction and control of air operations directly supporting the ground combat element. It processes and coordinates requests for immediate air support and coordinates air missions requiring integration with ground forces and other supporting arms. It normally collocates with the senior fire support coordination center within the ground combat element and is subordinate to the tactical air command center. Also called **DASC**. (JP 1-02)

electronic attack—Division of electronic warfare involving the use of electromagnetic energy, directed energy, or antiradiation weapons to attack personnel, facilities, or equipment with the intent of degrading, neutralizing, or destroying enemy combat capability and is considered a form of fires. Also called **EA**. (JP 1-02)

electronic warfare—Military action involving the use of electromagnetic and directed energy to control the electromagnetic spectrum or to attack the enemy. Also called **EW**. (JP 1-02)

electronic warfare support—Division of electronic warfare involving actions tasked by, or under direct control of, an operational commander to search for, intercept, identify, and locate or localize sources of intentional and unintentional radiated electromagnetic energy for the purpose of immediate threat recognition, targeting, planning and conduct of future operations. Also called **ES**. (JP 1-02)

fire support coordination center—A single location in which are centralized communications facilities and personnel incident to the coordination of all forms of fire support. Also called **FSCC**. (JP 1-02)

forward air controller—An officer (aviator/pilot) member of the tactical air control party who, from a forward ground or airborne position, controls aircraft in close air support of ground troops. Also called **FAC**. (JP 1-02)

identification—1. The process of determining the friendly or hostile character of an unknown detected contact. (JP 1-02, part 1 of a 3-part definition)

identification, friend or foe—A device that emits a signal positively identifying it as a friendly. Also called **IFF**. (JP 1-02)

joint operation—An operation carried on by a force that is composed of significant elements of the Army, the Navy or the Marine Corps, and the Air Force, or two or more of these Services operating under a single commander authorized to exercise unified command or operational control over joint forces. (*Note:* A Navy/Marine Corps operation is not a joint operation.) (MCRP 5-12C)

joint operations—A general term to describe military actions conducted by joint forces and those Service forces employed in specified command relationships with each other, which of themselves, do not establish joint forces. (JP 1-02)

maneuver warfare—A warfighting philosophy that seeks to shatter the enemy's cohesion through a variety of rapid, focused, and unexpected actions that create a turbulent and rapidly deteriorating situation with which the enemy cannot cope. (MCRP 5-12C)

Marine air command and control system—(See JP 1-02 for core definition. Marine Corps amplification follows.) The two major types of control exercised by the Marine air command and control system are air direction and air control. Also called **MACCS**. (MCRP 5-12C)

near real time—Pertaining to the timeliness of data or information which has been delayed by the time required for electronic communication and automatic data processing. This implies that there are no significant delays. Also called **NRT**. (JP 3-0)

positive control—(See JP 1-02 for core definition. Marine Corps amplification follows.) The tactical control of aircraft by a designated control unit, whereby the aircraft receives orders affecting its movements that immediately transfer responsibility for the safe navigation of the aircraft to the unit issuing such orders. (MCRP 5-12C)

procedural control—A method of airspace control that relies on a combination of previously agreed and promulgated orders and procedures. (JP 1-02)

remotely piloted vehicle—An unmanned vehicle capable of being controlled from a distant location through a communication link. It is normally designed to be recoverable. Also called **RPV**. (AAP-06)

rules of engagement—Directives issued by competent military authority that delineate the circumstances and limitations under which United States forces will initiate and/or continue combat engagement with other forces encountered. Also called **ROE**. (JP 1-02)

supporting arms—Weapons and weapons systems of all types employed to support forces by indirect or direct fire. (JP 1-02)

suppression of enemy air defenses—Activity that neutralizes, destroys, or temporarily degrades surface-based enemy air defenses by destructive and/or disruptive means. Also called **SEAD**. (JP 1-02)

tactical air command center—The principal US Marine Corps air command and control agency from which air operations and air defense warning functions are directed. It is the senior agency of the US Marine air command and control system that serves as the operational command post of the aviation combat element commander. It provides the facility from which the aviation combat element commander and his battle staff plan, supervise, coordinate, and execute all current and future air operations in support of the Marine air-ground task force. The tactical air command center can provide integration, coordination, and direction of joint and combined air operations. Also called **Marine TACC**. (MCWP 3-25)

tactical air operations center—The principal air control agency of the US Marine air command and control system responsible for airspace control and management. It provides real-time surveillance, direction, positive control, and navigational assistance for friendly aircraft. It performs real-time direction and control of all antiair warfare operations, to include manned interceptors and surface-to-air weapons. It is subordinate to the tactical air command center. Also called **Marine TAOC**. (JP 1-02)

target acquisition—The detection, identification, and location of a target in sufficient detail to permit the effective employment of weapons. Also called **TA**. (JP 1-02)

unmanned aircraft—An aircraft that does not carry a human operator and is capable of flight with or without human remote control. Also called **UA**. (JP 1-02)

unmanned aircraft system—That system whose components include the necessary equipment, network, and personnel to control an unmanned aircraft. Also called **UAS**. (JP 1-02)

REFERENCES AND RELATED PUBLICATIONS

Joint Publications (JPs)

1	Doctrine for the Armed Forces of the United States
3-30	Command and Control of Joint Air Operations
3-52	Joint Airspace Control

Chief of Naval Operations Instructions (OPNAVINSTs)

3710.7	Naval Air Training and Operating Procedures Standardization General Flight and Operating Instructions

NATO Standardization Agreements (STANAGs)

4586	Standard Interfaces of UAV Control Systems (UCS) for NATO UAV Interoperability

Marine Corps Publications

Marine Corps Warfighting Publications (MCWPs)

2-1	Intelligence Operations
2-21	Imagery Intelligence
3-2	Aviation Operations

Marine Corps Reference Publications (MCRP)

3-16D	Multi-Service Tactics, Techniques, and Procedures for Dynamic Targeting
3-25B	Multi-Service Brevity Codes
3-42.1A	Multi-Service Tactics, Techniques, and Procedures for the Tactical Employment of Unmanned Aircraft Systems

Miscellaneous Publications

Naval Tactics, Techniques, and Procedures 3-22.3-VMU, Combat Aircraft Fundamentals VMU
Concept of Operations for Marine Air-Ground Task Force Electronic Warfare
Concept of Operations for United States Marine Corps Family of Unmanned Aircraft Systems

www.ingramcontent.com/pod-product-compliance
Lightning Source LLC
Chambersburg PA
CBHW080441290526
45791CB00008BA/2573